Praise

'I have had the privilege both of meeting Jenny and also visiting Karis House. This book is filled with practical wisdom that is bringing help and hope to a growing number of young women. It represents years of hard work and sacrifice springing from deep-rooted compassion. This unashamedly flows from a belief that the Christian good news message offers freedom and the possibility of new beginnings for all.'

— **Stuart Bell**, Senior Pastor of Alive Church, Lincoln, and the leader of The Ground Level Network

'In these days where immediacy seems to have taken on an obsessional status, it's remarkable to read a book that re-affirms the reality that true transformation takes time! Time to become aware of the personal need for change and restoration, before rushing in to theorise the needs of others. This book is about Godly process. It speaks of how it may be true that "hurt people hurt people", it's equally powerful that "healed people heal people"! I commend this story of hope over despair. I once wrote about being "A dreamer for the Kingdom... dreams that will change a world that's lost its way" – Jenny is both a dreamer and a tireless activist.'

— **Rev Canon Chris Bowater OSL**, Pastor, worship leader, songwriter, author

'Excellent insightful book into helping people understand their struggles, well-structured and easily readable. If the reader engages with the journey and completes the steps suggested it will have a positive impact on their thinking, helping them to make sense of the "why" and give them a "how to" perspective of their future. The author clearly identifies the issues and walks with the readers throughout using examples of others who have walked the journey before. It brings hope into the hopelessness that some may feel about their situation and offers self-help suggestions which have worked for others.'

    — **Marion Sandhu**, Pastor of The Lighthouse Church

We're All a Little Bit Broken

Journey From Hurting To Healing

Jenny Tedbury

R^ethink

First published in Great Britain in 2020
by Rethink Press (www.rethinkpress.com)

Although all true, some of the names and circumstances in
the book have been changed to protect identities, families and
friends.

I dedicate this book to my loving, patient husband Mike and beautiful, talented daughter Elisabeth. You are my world and without either of you I would be a very different person. Thank you for your encouragement while I have been writing this book and the unwavering support you offer, whatever crazy scheme I dream up. I love you both with all my heart, now and forever.

Contents

Introduction   1

   Consider, Discover, Recover   7

   STEP UP actions   9

PART ONE Consider What Formed You   11

1 **Who Am I?**   13

   Upbringing   15

   Loss   21

   Abuse   23

   Peer pressure   30

   Bad personal choices   32

   Social media   35

   Summary   36

   STEP UP actions   37

2 **Why Do I Feel Like This?**   39

   Low self-worth   40

   Guilt and shame   44

Overthinking and anxiety 46

Anger 48

Mood swings 51

Nightmares and PTSD flashbacks 53

Summary 56

STEP UP actions 57

3 **What Do Other People See?** **59**

Trust 61

Unlovable 65

Relationships 69

Belonging 72

Comparison 75

Summary 78

STEP UP actions 79

PART TWO Discover How You Manage **83**

4 **How Do I Cope?** **85**

The mask 86

People pleasing 89

Building walls 91

Manipulation 93

Control 99

Self-harming 101

Substance misuse 104

Summary 106

STEP UP actions 107

5 What Else Impacts My Thinking?   **109**

Perspective   109

Attitude   112

Bullying   117

Personality type   119

Unforgiveness   127

Regret   130

Summary   131

STEP UP actions   132

PART THREE Recover The Real You   **135**

6 How Do I Become Me?   **137**

Understanding   138

Overcoming   140

Forgiveness   147

Reconciliation   153

Summary   157

STEP UP actions   158

7 Where Do I Go Now?   **161**

Acceptance   161

Belonging   167

Freedom   168

Growth   174

Transformation   175

Summary   179

STEP UP actions   180

Conclusion   183

Who Am I In Christ?   187

Just A Thought...   191

Acknowledgements   197

The Author   203

Introduction

When I was sixteen, I ran away from home. I was confused and upset. I didn't feel like I belonged there and thought that they would all be better off if I went. Anyway, I didn't know what else to do, so I ran. It turned out that I didn't belong anywhere else either. Wherever I found myself I would really try to fit in, behaving like everyone else, working hard to be useful so they would want me, but after a while in each place it was always the same – I felt like I didn't really belong.

With all this fitting in, I completely lost sight of me, of who I had been. Although I'm not sure I ever really knew who that was in the first place. This sense of being different, unwanted and rejected stayed on in the background, just under the surface. Looking back, it impacted almost everything I did, although at the time I had no idea why I felt so bad – I just did.

I developed many ways to cope with how I felt. I was the joker, the funny one, the life and soul of any party. I smoked and drank to excess to hide the pain and to give myself a break from the unrelenting sense of not being enough. I had many friends, but they were all superficial relationships because I didn't dare let anyone see the real me in case they ran. That left me very lonely; I could sit in a roomful of people and still feel totally isolated.

After nights out drinking with friends, where I would be right in the middle of it all, I would then return to my room alone and the deep sadness would take over. There were times when it was so overwhelming that I would sit on the window ledge and consider throwing myself to the ground. The only thing that stopped me was the fear that I would fail to die and be paralysed, dependent on others for the rest of my life. It stood to reason that I would mess this up; after all, I didn't get anything else right.

Day to day I lived my life with the damage hidden from view, but it directed my every move. While progressing through all the normal life stages of marriage, child, divorce, bereavement, remarriage and professional training, I was dogged by this rejection issue, this continual insecurity and sense of not being good enough. There was some brief respite and an easing of that feeling when I gave birth to my beautiful daughter. She was so perfect – how could I not be good enough? Then I next briefly lost the insecurity when I married again. Being with my amazing new husband in our lovely home made me feel safe, but the pattern had already been set.

I was still a perfectionist and could not allow myself to fail at anything. Had my first husband not been a violent alcoholic I would never have allowed that marriage to fail. At work I was ruthless and ambitious to get to the top. If I was unacceptable to most people just for being me, I would become worthy through my success, so I worked tirelessly to prove that I had value. Eventually it all became too much; the weight of the mismatch between how I felt on the inside versus how differently I behaved on the outside caught up with me. I became totally overwhelmed, unable to manage the pretence alone any longer.

It was in my despair and hopelessness over this that God entered my life in a very real way. I had already been attending church for some years, but for the first time God became personal to me. He entered my heart and instantly showed me that He loved me unconditionally. This personal encounter shifted my values in a moment and my recovery from all the pain and hurt of the past began. This journey changed me so dramatically that I knew it could do the same for others. I wanted others to be able to change their thinking as I had done; to give up struggling alone, trying to make sense of their thoughts, and to let God help. I knew there were girls out there who felt like I had years before, and who needed to know what I knew now, and so the idea for Karis House was born.

Nearly ten years later, with the full support of my husband and daughter, my dream finally became a reality. We opened Karis House, a recovery home for young women with issues that are controlling how they live, as mine did. Some of these girls are functioning outwardly but hurting greatly inside. Others have been unable to function even in day-to-day living and are trapped at home or in cycles of self-harm, addictions, eating disorders or anxiety. The outworkings of inner pain are numerous.

Karis is a residential supported living environment where the girls can explore their emotions in a safe place. They work in a structured God-centred programme that helps them journey to healing and recovery. As we walk with them through their past, they *consider* and deal with things that have damaged them or continue to cause them harm. They are helped to *discover* and understand some of the ways they behave today, especially the coping mechanisms they use in the belief that they keep them safe. They are shown new, less harmful ways to *recover* who they really are. They leave Karis able to function in ways they could not have dreamed of before. You will hear about some of them as you read on through the book, although their names and some details have been changed to protect their privacy.

So many things can impact us throughout our lives, some we don't even remember and others we can never forget, that it can be hard to pinpoint where we lost sight of ourselves. That process, though, whether in a horrible moment or over a much slower period, can erode our beliefs, confidence, security and self-esteem to the point that we can no longer access who we started out as. When we lose sight of who we were it's incredibly hard to grow into the person we wanted to become.

While I set up Karis to give young women a haven in which to work through their issues, I don't believe that the only way you can do this is by living in supported accommodation. I didn't do this myself, nor would it have been practical for me at the time. There are many people like me, who carry some pain from their past that they don't know how to process, but who could not manage to spend time in a residential setting. If you are one of those people, reading this book will help you, or maybe you know someone who still has internal struggles with something in their past and you could help them by sharing this book with them. Whether we know it or not, we're all a little bit broken.

I've written this book because helping people to understand God's amazing ability to love us regardless of our past has become my passion. I want everyone to understand that they are loved unconditionally when they ask God into their hearts and lives. He will guide them to freedom, whether that is a miracle healing in the moment or over a period of time spent unravelling the past. He can achieve either, and I have seen both happen.

This book has been written from the heart. It is a personal insight from many years of experience and working with people. I write predominantly as the founding chief executive of Karis House, but I also have experience previously as a nurse, Assistant Director of Public Health for Lincolnshire Health Authority, and church youth leader. Currently I am a church leader, wife, mother, grandmother and friend... and I have two dogs.

If you don't know God for yourself yet or if your relationship with Him is a bit distant, I invite you to pray this prayer with me before you start your journey. If you don't feel ready for that yet, that's fine too – maybe come back here later. Knowing that He is right by your side will give you all you need to succeed on your healing journey to recovery.

Lord Jesus Christ, I am sorry for the things I have done wrong in my life. I ask your forgiveness and now turn from everything which I know is wrong. Thank you for dying on the Cross for me to set me free from my sins. Please come into my life and fill me with your Holy Spirit and be with me forever. Thank you, Lord Jesus. Amen.

'Do not conform to the pattern of this world but be transformed by the renewing of your mind.'

— Romans 12:2[1]

Consider, Discover, Recover

The book is written in three sections: **Consider**, **Discover** and **Recover**. These will show the steps we travel with the girls at Karis and I invite you to come along too. I will be your companion as you embark on your transformational healing journey, but much more than that, God will be with you all the way.

Consider: In this section of the book we will consider all that may have impacted our lives. In Chapter One we will consider the events that may have formed us. In Chapter Two we will consider some of the negative outcomes of these events. In the final chapter in this section we will consider our relationships with others.

Discover: Once we move to this section, we will discover how we may have reacted in our lives to the events outlined in the first part of the book. In Chapter Four we will discover some of the coping strategies

---

1   Scriptures taken from the Holy Bible, New International Version®, NIV®. Copyright © 1973, 1978, 1984, 2011 by Biblica, Inc.™ Used by permission of Zondervan. All rights reserved worldwide. www. zondervan.com. The 'NIV' and 'New International Version' are trademarks registered in the United States Patent and Trademark Office by Biblica, Inc.®

we may have used to manage life. In Chapter Five we will discover a range of other ways we might regard the impact on our lives of the events outlined in the previous chapters.

Recover: The first two sections of the book should identify areas to work on with God as you go. Now we are going to recover the real you. In Chapter Six, you will find ways to recover who you were always meant to be. We will finish in Chapter Seven by looking at where you go now. How do you hold on to your growth and transformation and fulfil the amazing dreams that God has placed in your heart?

There is a lot to cover in the first two parts of the book and obviously not all we talk about will apply to you. At the end of each chapter you will have the opportunity to take a break to do the STEP UP actions. They are like a little oasis that will allow you time for reflection and to draw close to God. It will be a moment for you to stop, rest and process what you have just read, although some actions will be harder for you than others. You may need to repeat some of the STEP UP actions if there is more than one area in a chapter that is relevant to your life – you need to explore them all.

STEP UP actions

Spend time with God

Think about what you've just read

Explore the relevance to you

Pray about it

Uncover scriptures that speak to you

Personal journal

It would be a great idea to begin a new personal journal alongside this book. You can write in it every time you have a thought connected to your journey and while carrying out your STEP UP actions. Write in scriptures that come to mind from God or that other people give you as you are travelling this journey. Read your personal journal as you go along; it will encourage you to see your progress and how your thinking is changing. It will also show you how far you have come at the end of your journey.

The Cambridge Dictionary definition of 'step up' is 'to take action where there is a need or opportunity for it'.² You decide where there is a need for you to step up and *take action*, and I will provide the *opportunity*.

Only you can decide whether you are ready or willing to take up the opportunity this book provides. I sincerely hope that you will.

> 'Ask and it will be given to you; seek and you will find; knock and the door will be opened to you. For everyone who asks receives; the one who seeks finds; and to the one who knocks, the door will be opened.'
> — Matthew 7:7–8

---

2   (n.d.) 'step up', Cambridge Dictionary Online, https://dictionary. cambridge.org/dictionary/english/step-up

PART ONE
CONSIDER WHAT FORMED YOU

Part One will begin your healing journey by considering the many things that can impact our lives negatively, whether we are aware of them or not.

1
Who Am I?

If I asked, 'Who are you?' what would your answer be? Do you know or would that question throw you out completely? Would you know but be embarrassed to say? Or are you just lost, uncertain of who you are because you have spent so long fitting in with others? Has your lack of confidence or fear of failure made you afraid to give your opinion in case you are judged unfavourably? Is there something in your past that left you reeling and caused you to lose sight of who you were or who you wanted to become and, if so, do you know what that was? So many things happen as we grow and learn – many are normal and positive, whereas others are far from either. What we do know is that all of them eventually have an impact on who we become, even if they didn't seem that big a deal at the time, or we have no memory of them now.

We will also meet some of the girls who have been at Karis House and learn how their past impacted their lives before they came to us and how God has brought them through.

Almost without exception, the girls who come to us at Karis cannot answer the question, 'Who are you?' Usually they feel they lost sight of that many years ago, if they ever knew it at all. Few of them know who they want to become, either, with some of them not even sure if they have or deserve a future. This breaks my heart and reminds me of where I came from, too. In knowing that, though, I can be certain that if they want it badly enough there is a better future for them, and for you too if you are in that place today.

Let's begin this chapter by looking at some of the events that can happen to us throughout our lives and by starting to consider the things that have contributed to who we have become. We will revisit some of the negative events in our lives that might have bruised us or formed deep wounds. We will also consider how even normal parenting can have a negative impact if the way that love was given did not connect in the way we needed to receive it. There are some circumstances that can impact us that are no one's fault, such as the order in which we were born in the family. It's clear that many things in both childhood and adulthood come together to form us and our beliefs.

I want to start the journey by looking at how we get to where we are right now; what kinds of things impacted us and made us the people we are today?

Upbringing

The first thing to impact who we become is obviously our upbringing. There has been much debate over the years over which is the driving force: nature or nurture. Many feel that nature – the genetics we carry from our parents coupled with our innate personalities – is what determines the outcome. Others are proponents of the nurture theory, which says that we are fully shaped by our environment. Still others believe that in reality it is a mixture of both. Personally, I'm in agreement with the last of these; we are the product of who we were born as, combined with how we are brought up and our home environment.

In today's society, family can mean many different things other than simply a mum, a dad and 2.4 kids. We have such a range of family set-ups now that I dare not list them for fear of causing offence by missing someone's core family out. Needless to say, the notion of 'normal' is wide and varied, so how can we deny that this has an impact on people as they grow up? There is much research on how young people in the care system – fostering or children's homes – often do not achieve as much as their counterparts who are living with birth parents. This supports the theory that more than just genetics must come into play when we consider potential outcomes for children.

It has also been shown that divorce is more prevalent among people whose own parents were divorced. In our homes for previously homeless young people, many of our youngsters have come from homes where the parent has a new partner and this has caused disharmony within the family, especially when the parent has been on their own for a while, as jealousies can be rife. Sadly, when parents are faced with a 'him / her or me' scenario they often choose the new part- ner over their teenage children. They may perceive that their child is now old enough to manage without them or will be leaving the family home soon anyway, or they may simply be fearful of having to manage alone again.

SALLY

Sally and her siblings had been on their own with Mum since they could remember, but then Mum got a new boyfriend. This was tricky to begin with but eventually they settled into a reasonable new routine in the home. Sally found him more difficult to live with than her sisters did; she felt he picked on her a lot. Mum didn't agree with Sally's viewpoint on this and they started to argue too. This seemed to give the new boyfriend renewed vigour for the fight and he increased his negative behaviour towards Sally. She felt that she and Mum arguing gave him the right to attack her more, because he could see that if she complained, Mum took his side.

Things got worse and worse and eventually Sally, although in her early teens, decided she couldn't go on living that way anymore. Even knowing Sally was leaving didn't alter Mum's point of view; she still didn't accept that Sally was being constantly abused by the boyfriend, who by all accounts was clever at how he set about it. As a young teenager Sally was no match for the devious older man in this fight. She left home and began to spiral out of control. This maternal rejection was the start of many years of abnormal coping behaviours for Sally, as we will hear as we go along, until she finally ended up with us at Karis House in her late twenties.

This type of rejection can lay the foundation for lifelong bitterness, insecurity, trust issues and low self-esteem in the now homeless young person. Additionally, there can be substantial damage from maternal deprivation which causes them to get into a cycle of constantly seeking attention and affection, and a desire for a family situation. While girls suffer more overtly, it can affect boys too. This will take them in repeating circles for much of their life as they fight to meet this need in inappropriate ways and situations, some exceedingly dangerous and damaging.

This maternal deprivation can occur for many other reasons; the mother doesn't have to be absent for it to happen. Some mothers don't know how to parent and others just don't want to. At other times the way a mother loves her child is not how the child receives love and so they do not *feel* loved. This is a bit like throwing a ball at a bat but missing – the throw still takes place even if the ball does not hit the bat. Sometimes love is shown but it does not hit the mark, leaving a lasting sense of rejection and damage.

Either way, the child is left unfulfilled and searches for love later, maybe in inappropriate places. People give and receive love in different ways; this is explained clearly in *The 5 Love Languages* by Gary Chapman.[3] He identifies the primary ways he believes that people perceive love as quality time, words of affirmation, gifts, acts of service and physical touch. He and Ross Campbell then adapt this in a further book for parents to be able to recognise these needs in their children and give them love or attention in the manner they require.[4] They explore how this works in practice very well.

Missing a father or a father's love can also be damaging. The father is expected to be responsible for provision and protection; when this is missing from the father in a family, or the father is missing altogether, it can leave the child feeling uncertain of how to get their needs met and they may feel unsafe. They may feel that they have to become very capable in life as they need to protect themselves, even if the mother has stepped into that role. With only one parent, the

---

3   G Chapman, *The 5 Love Languages* (Moody Publishers, 2015)
4   G Chapman and R Campbell, *The 5 Love Languages of Children: The secret to loving children effectively* (Moody Publishers, 2016)

safety of a family unit is missing, which may also create a need to belong somewhere secure, or to create that family unit in adulthood for their own children. For girls, their father is also the first male relationship where they learn to relate differently, and for boys, they miss the role model.

A poor father experience can make it harder for some people to relate to a loving Father God as they align Him with the negative parenting of their own father. This can cause some unusual issues. If your father left your life for whatever reason, this can make you feel that God will do the same. If you don't trust your father, it will be difficult to trust God. When your father is present in your life but distant, and the relationship between you is poor, it's much less likely that you can believe that your relationship with a Father God can be a good one. He will probably feel distant too, unless you become aware of the root cause and understand why.

People often grumble about the order they were born into the family. The eldest child may be jealous of subsequent children, having had the parents to themselves for a period. They may consider themselves used because they have to look after younger siblings, whether or not they actually do. The middle children often feel insignificant, overlooked because they were not the special firstborn and nor are they the baby of the family who, they think, gets all the attention. The youngest can expect life to go on providing everything they want with minimal effort and become frustrated when life doesn't work that way. Maybe everyone else in the family won't allow them to grow up, even when they are no longer children. These things can be real or just perceived; either way, they can leave a lasting legacy and affect how we respond in the future.

In earlier times families used to live near other relatives and often stayed in the same area throughout their lives. These days, people are more on the move. It's not unusual for the whole family to be uprooted and moved to wherever Mum or Dad want or need to work. The term 'uprooted' gives us a little insight into the potential for harm in this. When we uproot plants, we quite literally rip their life-sustaining roots out of their environment and unless we nurture them carefully during the transition into their new home they will die, or at the very least their growth will be stunted. Sometimes parents underestimate the potential damage that can be caused to children and young people by being moved during school age. Changing schools and losing local support networks to work through the grief of this loss can be incredibly hard for them.

I vividly remember being moved in my last year at primary school and then again three years into my secondary education. The village primary school I moved into was tiny compared with my previous school and everyone in all the years knew everyone else. I was an outsider and felt exactly that. I was alone for that whole last year. Arriving at secondary school I was cautious, afraid to make friends in case we moved again, although my parents gave no hint that this was on the cards. Eventually I settled and made friends, good friends. I was in the centre of everything and loving school life. Then came the bombshell. We were moving again, even further away this time. There was absolutely no opportunity for me to maintain connections with this new solid base of good, trustworthy friends who wanted me around. I was devastated. It felt like something in me broke that day.

Loss

Grief from losing friendships can be damaging but losing a parent or sibling will be greater still. The effects can include all those listed previously plus total confusion at the sudden and permanent loss of a parent. Unless handled well by the remaining parent, who of course will be grieving themselves in this circumstance, the child may suffer lasting damage from this trauma. Even when a child is given all the appropriate help and support, this incident may still result in abnormal coping mechanisms for a long time to come, if not forever.

Into adulthood, there is also the potential damage from a miscarriage or losing a child. The death of a child has the added sorrow of being unexpected; losing a parent in adulthood is devastating but is the natural order of things, so while upsetting, it is somewhat expected. The death of a child, though, is not. This is an obviously distressing and incredibly difficult situation to come to terms with and those unfortunate enough to find themselves in that position have a hard task moving forward at all, let alone doing so and overcoming their grief to live productively.

Bereavement brings a pain like no other, but, like invisible physical illness, others can't see it. If the people around you are unaware of your situation, they can seem insensitive to your pain and you can feel totally isolated. There is also a real difficulty in our culture with handling death. People just don't know what to say to you, or how to broach the subject, so instead they say nothing. Sometimes the bereaved person is longing to talk about the person they have lost but they sense that others are uncomfortable with this and so say nothing, suffering in silence. This can breed deep feelings of resentment which are never addressed and go on to produce all manner of problems, sometimes even physical illness.

Earlier we touched on the damage from a miscarriage. Sometimes the loss is not an actual physical pregnancy or child but finding out that there can never be one. Many young women assume that a baby will become a part of their life without actively planning how or when. Still others long for that occurrence. Some of these dreams will never be fulfilled for myriad reasons. When this reality hits it can be a devastating loss, compounded by a lack of understanding from some of those around them. Well-meaning friends can make inappropriate suggestions in their desire to fix the situation. These, in some instances, can cause almost as much damage as the knowledge of a future without children.

The flip side to this is young women who find themselves pregnant when childbearing was never part of their life plan. They can be left mourning the loss of their independence, or their current role. If termination is chosen, despite not wanting children they may feel guilt or shame and even the loss of the child.

Many people experience all the symptoms of grief in a broken relationship or divorce situation. In addition to the loss of the partner is the immense sadness at the loss of the planned future life with this person. There could also be a loss of the family home, shared friendship groups and, for some, daily contact with their children.

Abuse

Whatever age you are, the impact of abuse is immense. It has the effect of depersonalising you so that in the eyes of the abuser you are purely there to serve their needs. This has the power to diminish you as a person to the point that, with ongoing abuse, you can come to believe the abuser's viewpoint and see yourself as there to serve them, with no value of your own. Some abuse victims even come to believe the abuse is actually their fault for being ugly, weak, stupid or simply bad, which is clearly untrue, but believing it can have extremely negative effects in the moment and far into the future.

Abuse can cover a varied range of behaviours – verbal, physical, emotional, spiritual and sexual. The impact is as varied as the behaviours themselves but is generally long lasting. Some factors that come into play are how long the abuse goes on for and how old we are when the abuse takes place. How someone is treated if they disclose abuse can be pivotal to how that person will see themselves after the event. Some children cannot begin to see a way out when suffering abuse regularly in the home, but research has shown that they will keep quiet about it to protect the safety of the family unit, choosing to stay living with the abuser rather than being removed. They accept the known, however horrible, rather than risking the loss of a parent or home environment.

LISA

When one of our girls, Lisa, in her teens, finally told her adoptive mother she was being abused by her adoptive father, the mother told her that was just how he showed he loved her. This devastated her emotionally because she wasn't offered the protection she expected from her adoptive mother. Additionally, the abuse sadly continued.

To Lisa it seemed that his and the rest of the family's needs were more important than hers. She felt unable to speak out about it again for a long time, assuming anyone else would dismiss it in the same way, and was fearful of her and her siblings having no home.

Eventually she could cope no longer and shared her situation with a social worker, but the family managed to convince the social worker that it wasn't true, so she backed down. Finally, as soon as she was old enough, she left her adopted home.

Sexual abuse can occur within the family unit or outside. Although within the family there is a higher chance that it will become an ongoing situation, this can also be the case in other situations like school or work. Many people experience a one-off incident, for example being rubbed up against inappropriately on a train, which is at the very least unpleasant. Then there are more frightening sexual attacks which often carry a threat of violence, like rape. While these may be one-off events, their impact can be devastating and have far reaching consequences.

All of these situations cause varying degrees of damage dependent on the time, place and where someone is emotionally at the time. How someone responds during the abuse and how people close to them respond when the victim shares can have a lasting impact. Many factors determine the level of current and ongoing harm following sexual abuse.

Emotional abuse cannot always be recognised at first, sometimes even by the one being abused. The term 'gaslighting' was coined following the 1938 stage play *Gas Light* and its subsequent screen adaptations, in which a woman is made to feel she is losing her mind by her new husband, who wants to have her committed so he can take advantage of her wealth. He repeatedly alters the level of the gaslights in the house and denies making any changes to convince her she has lost clarity. This form of abuse erodes the person's ability to trust themselves and make decisions; they can become convinced after a while that they are in the wrong. The abuser then takes control more easily as they are 'helping out' with things that the abused can supposedly no longer handle. An additional misfortune here is that the abuser soon loses respect for the person they've hoodwinked, but generally carries on using them and making their lives miserable. With the loss of confidence there is little chance of a way out for the abused person unless perceptive friends or family members recognise the pattern of abuse.

This kind of progressive undermining can also be evident in physical abuse situations. This, of course, tends to be coupled with fear of the next violent outburst. In this circumstance the abused will work hard to appease the abuser to reduce the risk of upsetting them. They will attempt to stay ahead of and attend to every need that person may have, sometimes even before the abuser is aware of the need. In this way the abused person diminishes the chances of violence, but this can be at great cost to their own health, both during this time and long after they are free, with these behaviours unconsciously occurring in other ongoing day-to-day situations with others.

Spiritual abuse can include a church leader using their position to shame or control their congregation members, or by creating a toxic culture within the church. Biblical scripture may be used to manipulate people to act in a way that is beneficial to the leader. It can be difficult to identify, as mentioned above, because people may be unaware of it. The leader may, in courting popularity, choose influential people or friends for key roles to gain their favour to the detriment of others. This can leave others feeling confused and despondent that their best efforts aren't good enough.

Spiritual abuse can also occur when an abusive partner insults or ridicules a person's spiritual beliefs or uses their faith to manipulate them. They can stop them from practising the faith at all or prevent the children being raised in that faith. In other situations, they may insist that the children are brought up in a particular faith against their partner's will. All of these actions can be harmful because a person's spiritually is personal to them.

Verbal abuse, often thought to be a much lesser event than other forms of abuse, is what people say to us or about us. It's important to recognise that the long-term effects can sometimes be incredibly damaging.

Commonly on the programme at Karis we hear girls reporting back what parents said to or about them that has stuck with them and prevented them from attempting things or led them to actively live up or down to something a parent said many years previously. In many cases you know that the parent would be horrified to think that their off-the-cuff comment would continue to have such an impact on their child, yet it does. Often worse than the odd comment can be the comparison between children, made innocently or in frustration; this can burn deep in the child's heart and remain well into adulthood. 'She's not as academic as her brother' can send a girl into a frenzy of lifelong study to prove otherwise, or lead her to determine in her heart that she is hopeless at studying and make her give up on it there and then and to avoid it for the rest of her life. Neither of these is a good outcome, especially when based on comments that may be passing or 'in the moment' with no hidden agenda or real thought behind them.

A teacher can also deliver the kind of comment that can alter a child's course in life. Many people remember a teacher telling them they were rubbish in their subject and so steer away from anything to do with that subject for life.

A teacher once told me my accent was terrible when I spoke French. To this day, while I understand French well enough, I rarely speak it. Even knowing that the root cause of this reticence is unreasonable, it put a big question mark over my ability in this area and I struggle to move past it. I have to say at this point that my husband speaks fluent French, so there's not much need for me to do so anyway… and yes, I know that's just an excuse. So here I'm really speaking to myself. I've given myself permission to let that teacher's words have a lasting impact, even though I know they were insignificant (my husband says my accent's fine).

Sometimes it isn't the words others say about us, it's what we say about ourselves. 'Oh, I'm rubbish, stupid, clumsy…' The list could go on and on. We can be our own biggest critics – well, if you're anything like me you can. We say these things without even thinking about it, but we repeat them constantly. When we speak these negative words about our lives, who hears them the most? We do, of course, because we are always with us. If we repeat negative things about ourselves constantly, in time we will come to believe them without even thinking about it. We speak them with our mouths, and they come back around and in through our ears and eventually take root in our hearts. Then they become our new reality. Someone once said, 'Our words shape our world,' and it's true. If we keep saying we're rubbish then, in time, we will come to believe it and that will limit what we might try to achieve, because we will have little faith in our 'rubbish' selves. If, however, we speak positive things into our hearts we will be able to achieve anything our hearts desire – within reason, of course.

Something else to consider here is that when we speak against ourselves, whom God made, we are speaking against God's perfect creation. No, I'm not saying we need to be perfect, but God made us that way to begin with and He wants us to be the best version of us we can be. If you had children, imagine how heartbroken you would be if you could hear them in their bedroom at night crying out how rubbish they were. Wouldn't you be thinking about all the great things you see in them and the wonderful future their personalities or gifts will give them? That's how God thinks about us; He made each one of us for a unique purpose, even if we haven't worked out what that is yet.

Peer pressure

We tend to think of peer pressure as something the young have to contend with, and it is true that what others in your age group think can have a massive influence in your teens. It's safe to say, however, that any peer group can hold sway over how we behave at any age, for example keeping up with the Joneses. There is an irony in the fact that young people profess to hate school uniform and all having to dress the same, but if you go anywhere that young people gather they are frequently hanging out in the same style blue jeans and wearing similar tops or hoodies; often, best mates dress almost identically. While not liking being told what to wear, when they get together they choose to dress alike, which seems to create a sense of belonging.

In reality, this doesn't stop after your teens; young mums come together and worry if their child doesn't appear to be reaching milestones at the same time as other people's children and may feel they are failing if the child appears behind. In the comparison trap, at whatever age, no one can win. Being measured, weighed up by the group and found wanting is everyone's ongoing nightmare. When my husband comes home with an invitation for us to somewhere I haven't been before and there's no dress code on the invitation I'm filled with worry. Who wants to turn up in jeans if it's a formal long-dress affair or vice versa? Being a man, he doesn't understand it when I pressure him to find out the dress code for the evening.

People need to belong. How they look, what they wear and how they behave allows them to be part of a specific group – or not. In many groups there will be the odd one who has such great self confidence that they will still remain part of the group, even if they don't conform. Ironically, many people are often envious of the one who doesn't mind standing out, because it's recognised that they are their own person and content with who and what they are. It's a sad indictment of our time that these unique people are few and far between. It's also sad that sometimes these different souls are picked on and bullied for being different, which persuades others that looking the same and behaving the same is generally the safest way forward in life. Unfortunately, some of these people are not actually as confident as it appears on the surface, but using a coping strategy. We will look more at these later in another chapter.

Bad personal choices

Having seen how important it is to feel like we belong, the next thing to consider is where we belong. To whom do we owe our allegiance? When we are young it is to our family, if we are fortunate enough to have one. At school things can get a little trickier. There is always a group of students who seem to delight in messing around and determine not to do schoolwork at all, or at least as little as they can get away with. If you make the personal choice to be a part of one of those groups, no matter how smart you are, your education is going to suffer. What you actually learn, or rather don't learn, in school can affect your choices into adulthood. Sadly, many students are too young to recognise this at the time and don't listen when it is pointed out by parents or teachers. Even if a decision is made to switch groups when the realisation sinks in, it may be too late to catch up and so you fall back into the old pattern.

HOLLY

One of our girls at Karis, Holly, had aligned herself with a disruptive group in school. By her own admission she was lazy, and this group celebrated such behaviour, so she was popular and happy in her comfort zone. She got a bit of a reputation for herself, which to begin with she was proud of. After a time, though, she realised that she was letting her parents down and that she would not be able to achieve what she wanted in life if she kept this up. She tried really hard to change her behaviour and switch groups but became isolated when no one trusted her. Her old group felt betrayed, so they bullied her, and the new groups she was trying to become part of didn't want her because they didn't feel they could trust her. It got so bad that one of the girls physically assaulted her. Her parents felt this was unacceptable so they moved the family to another town so that Holly could have a fresh start.

To begin with, things went OK at her new school. Unfortunately, as Holly began to make friends she fell back into using her old techniques; she said she wanted them to think that she was really cool. She thought people would find her boring if they got to know the real Holly, so she told stories of some of the negative things she used to get up to in her old school. She said she knew as soon as the words came out of her mouth that it was a stupid thing to do, but it was too late, the others had heard her bragging. She was beside herself for letting her parents down again. She felt worse because this was a Christian school and she knew the girls she wanted to be friends with weren't impressed by her old behaviours. Now she was falling back into old patterns of behaviour. The damage was already deep and an overwhelming anxiety set in. It got so bad that she could barely leave the house or be alone without her mother nearby.

Bad choices don't stop in our childhood. We can get involved with the wrong group of people at any time in life. When we mix with others who are negative, we become that way too. It's much easier to pull people down and takes a lot more effort to pull them up. People love gossip and talking about others. It's not easy to stand against the crowd, where you also take the risk of being grouped with the one they are talking about; it's easier to join in or keep quiet than defend or offer an opposing opinion. Many insecure people are mean and judgemental about others, hoping to make themselves look better by comparison. What they fail to realise is that in time people begin to wonder what is being said about them by that person when they are not around.

Peer pressure, as we discussed earlier, can find us drinking more than we can handle or taking drugs just to fit in even when we know it's not right for us. It's a fact that some people have a more addictive personality than others and they may find that they become addicted. Before they have realised it, that one bad choice has led to a lifetime of addiction with many more bad choices to follow.

Social media

Well, obviously everyone else leads a perfect life and it's just me who has not got it together. Am I the only one who feels this? I'm pretty sure that's not the case but it's quite hard work to remind yourself sometimes when you see everyone else posting from amazing places, looking totally perfect and smiling their socks off, isn't it? Yet in reality we all know these are just moments in time, and some of them aren't really even that. I saw a couple in a restaurant make about ten attempts at getting the perfect 'moment in time' selfie one evening, while their dinner was going cold. We have to remember that, for every selfie showing a fabulous moment, that person has just as many ordinary moments as anyone else. While many of us can see social media as a bit of fun, for some younger people it can be destructive. It is a perfect place for bullying, where one comment can grow and destroy someone's credibility as others jump on the bandwagon. It is an opportunity to bully or attack others with little responsibility attached. People will say things on social media they wouldn't dare say face to face. It is easy to post whatever you like without substantiating the facts. For young people it can add a whole new dimension where they are expected to perform well to meet peer pressure. The desire for 'likes' on their posts can become intense, almost addictive. Sadly, in the attempt to get the perfect post, some young people have lost their lives as the physical risks they are prepared to take increase.

We need to enjoy social media for what it should be seen as: a bit of fun and a way to connect with those from further afield. It has its place and in itself it isn't a problem – it's only what we choose to make it in our heads.

Summary

In this chapter we have begun to consider the things that have contributed to who we are today. We have looked at some of the many negative events in our life that might have bruised us and formed deep wounds. We have also considered how even normal parenting can have a negative impact if the way that love was given did not connect with the one receiving it. We looked at circumstances that also impact but are no one's fault, such as the order we were born in the family. It's clear, even from the few scenarios I've outlined here, that many things in both childhood and adulthood come together to form us and our beliefs.

'For You created my inmost being, You knit me together in my mother's womb.'
— Psalm 139:13

STEP UP actions

Spend time with God

Now is a good moment to spend some time with God. To do this, find a quiet space with no distractions and ask Him to bring to mind what He wants you to consider.

Think about what you've just read

Consider what we have covered here and perhaps things that you know impacted you, but which we haven't covered in this chapter.

Explore the relevance to you

Write down anything that you believe still impacts you. List both the negative and the positive things that have helped you to become who you are today.

Pray about it

Let's pray for God to prepare your heart to work to overcome any negative effects of these events. You can use the prayer below to get started or pray to God in your usual way, whichever feels most comfortable to you.

Father God, we know that You made us and that You love us the way we are, but that You love us too much to leave us that way. Be with me as I consider the events of my life that formed me up until now and help me to identify where I may need to make changes. Soften my heart, Lord, and allow me to be honest with myself. Thank you, Father. Amen.

Uncover scriptures that speak to you

Write scriptures on Post-it notes or coloured card and put them all around the house or in your pocket to support your journey.

Personal journal

Write about the outcomes in your personal journal to remind you just how far you've come on the days when you need encouragement.

2
Why Do I Feel Like This?

We've had a look at the things that can happen throughout our lives and how they might feed into our future, but how can our past impact us today? What possible effect can something that happened to us as a child, say, have on our day-to-day living now? Many people think they have no issues with anything that happened to them in their childhood or maybe following trauma, a breakup or bereavement, but it's surprising just what an effect these things might still be having without them realising the root cause. Some of our overwhelming emotions about something today may be connecting with something we felt in the past and magnifying it; sometimes we don't realise it and at other times we know about it but don't know how to deal with it. In this chapter we're going to explore more closely what kind of outcomes can result from our past experiences, from childhood or adult circumstances.

Low self-worth

A major beauty company had the advertising strapline 'because you're worth it', but what if you don't *feel* worth it? How do you cope with that? Some of the life experiences we talked about in the first chapter can leave our self-esteem in tatters. It's hard for anyone to believe that they have any worth if even their parents appear not to value them. Much of our self-esteem comes from our early interactions with our parents. How they treat us tells us whether we have value or not, firstly in the home and then out into the wider world. If a parent has chosen their current partner over us, or has walked out on the family, it might be reasonable to consider that we are of lower value to them. Their choice would indicate that we have low worth in their eyes. Girls have said to me, 'If even my mum or my dad don't want me then I must be rubbish because they created me – why would anyone else want to be with me if they don't?' It's a tricky logic to argue with.

While it's easy to see the disappointment and diminishing self-worth in having a parent choose someone else over you, it's harder to understand the loss of worth when it's the result of a parent's death, as death is rarely a deliberate decision. Let me tell you about Susie.

SUSIE

At the age of five Susie contracted chickenpox, which her mother then also caught. While Susie got over her chickenpox, her mother did not and became unwell – so ill that an ambulance came and took her to the hospital, where she fell into a coma. Susie was distressed that her mother was taken away without her having the opportunity to say goodbye and that no one told her at the time how ill her mother was or what was going on. While her mother remained in a coma there was hope she would eventually recover; however, Susie talks of an incident in which her mother was being bathed and her breathing tube fell out and she suffered irreversible brain damage.

Her father could not cope with Susie and her two younger siblings and began drinking heavily. The children were placed in the care of a much older couple who brought them up. While Susie blamed herself for giving her mother chickenpox she also suffered poor self-esteem, anxiety and depression over her mother and father leaving her, even though she knew her mother didn't leave on purpose or out of personal choice. Her father continued to drink heavily, seeing the children rarely, and died young when Susie was in her late teens. Two years later her mother also died.

Susie felt abandoned and rejected by both parents, even though she understood that her mother had had no choice. She felt worthless, that no one would ever want her around, and made many suicide attempts, which eventually led the couple who had brought her up to ask her to move out as the ongoing trauma was too much for them and her siblings. This just confirmed her lack of personal worth. Shortly after this she came to us at Karis to try to unpick the muddle she found her head was in.

Many people, like Susie, know the reality of a situation but still cannot process the information appropriately. While knowing that Mum leaving her was not deliberate and completely out of her own control, Susie still felt the emotions of abandonment. Despite having consistent, loving foster parents throughout her childhood, this did not eliminate the deep sense of rejection she felt from the loss of her mother's direct input in her life.

This emotional response deep within someone is not always recognised for what it is, especially when the person is saying all the right things out loud and appearing to others to fully comprehend their loss. That means that these emotions can become internalised and cause harm quietly until they become too overwhelming to cope with, the outcomes of which we will explore a little later in the book. Susie's foster parents were Christian, so she had gone to church as a child but struggled to believe God loved her because He had allowed such terrible things to happen to her. She didn't feel that it was ok to express this about God to her family because it seemed disrespectful. In addition to her deep-seated sense of rejection from her birth parents, she also felt rejected by God.

Another key reason for low self-esteem is as a response to abuse, either a one-off incident such as rape or ongoing abuse such as that which we spoke about in the first chapter. People underestimate how debilitating even a one-off incident can be long term, but that is a mistake. When someone is violated in this way the damage can be deep and, no matter how hard the person tries to put it behind them, it may show up in unexpected ways.

Ongoing abuse slowly removes all sense of self-worth until the abused person believes they have no worth and acts as if they expect to be mistreated. When someone feels they have little worth, they may become quiet or withdrawn, not pushing themselves forward for fear of more abuse or of being noticed. They don't want people to think that they expect anything. It can come across as humble or self-sacrificing but, in reality, they are worried about what other people think of them and whether they will notice they have been, or are being, abused.

The opposite behavioural outcome from ongoing abuse is that people get loud and over-the-top, excitable or angry. This reaction is about throwing people off the scent. Being funny makes others assume you are confident and happy; they will not notice the deep lack of self-worth. Being surly or super angry with everyone has a similar self-protective drive, as those around someone known to get angry stand back for fear of bearing the brunt of their anger. This behaviour may have an unexpected side effect of allowing the abused person to remain unknown and for the abuse to continue in some instances. Being bullied about weight or other personal status can cause people to make a joke of themselves before others do as another form of self-protection.

Guilt and shame

In most abusive situations, regardless of the form of abuse, the victim can feel to blame, that they have somehow created the situation. They often feel guilty and assume that something they have said or done has caused the abuser to be angry with them. They may feel ashamed because they believe they have been responsible for provoking their attacker by the way they are dressed or because they had too much to drink. The insecurity around their self-worth feeds into this false belief and often makes them isolated because of their shame in believing that they had a part to play in their situation. A sense of guilt, albeit based on misunderstanding, makes it harder to talk to anyone about what has happened, or an ongoing abusive situation.

In ongoing abuse, this is a perfect scenario for the abuser because they can play on this guilt and remain concealed for much longer, which is why the rates of domestic abuse continue to rise.

I remember being caught in a domestic abuse situation in my first marriage. I had divorced my husband for having affairs, being violent towards me and threatening towards my two-year-old daughter, much of which was caused by him drinking alcohol extensively. We left the area we lived in because of his unpredictable behaviour but after three years he tracked us down. He convinced me he had sobered up and was a changed man. I took him back against the advice of all my friends. I believed him because I really wanted it to be true, but he was more violent than ever and still drinking. I did not want to put my daughter through another change, so I stayed, hoping he would settle down. As time passed, I felt powerless to leave. Having gone against everyone's advice I was ashamed to discover how wrong I'd been in believing him and felt certain that I could not make good decisions anymore, so I stayed where I was. To begin with he did nothing in front of my daughter, but I had to keep my bruised arms covered from her and my friends. Despite normally being a strong, decisive woman, I felt increasingly powerless, too afraid and unable to change my appalling situation. I blamed myself for being stupid enough to believe him and guilty for putting my daughter in jeopardy.

Domestic abuse is hard to handle for all involved. The abuser has often come from a bad situation themselves, which in no way excuses it, but their sense of guilt or unfairness is distorted already, making it more difficult to reason with them. The abused can feel shame at being in the situation, especially if beforehand they saw themselves as capable and had strong views on how they thought they would behave under those conditions. I certainly never saw myself caught up in something that I wouldn't be strong enough to walk straight out of, as I'm pretty strong-willed, and yet it happened to me and has to many others. Sadly, it is a situation that still happens in many households today.

Overthinking and anxiety

These two are quite closely related; although you can have one without the other, more often than not over-thinking can lead to anxiety or vice versa. How many of us have lain in bed, tired but wide awake, thinking about a situation that has happened in the day, or that will likely happen tomorrow? Isn't it frustrating that we can't just do the logical, seemingly simple thing of going to sleep?

Not everyone suffers this way; my husband, for example, never worries in the night. As soon as the light is off, he is snoring almost instantly. Pretty unfair, I'd say. I, however, will attempt to understand the minutiae of the universe. I will worry and over-think conversations I've had or should have had that day and find myself anxious about how I'm going to handle some of the things coming up tomorrow. If my brain has considered something important, I struggle to control the desire to explore it from every angle and to try out a million different ways the conversation might go. Something in our pasts, probably alongside something in our personalities, will have created these different approaches.

HOLLY

When Holly was young, she worried constantly that her mother wasn't safe on her own. She couldn't remember what originally triggered this belief, but it was a strong belief and she was constantly afraid when her mother was out of the house alone that she wouldn't make it back safely. She would pester her dad to check on her mum, which he did for a while, then said he didn't need to do it anymore. Holly was distraught and made it her mission to always go with her mother when she was allowed.

Over time, this anxiety spread into other areas of Holly's life, to the point that by the time she came to Karis she could not spend long without her mother at all. She couldn't journey on public transport, but neither could she drive her car anywhere except her hometown. Initially she was trapped locally, but this soon became all-consuming and she was unable to go anywhere without her mum or a close friend. She even struggled being alone overnight, the anxiety and panic regularly overwhelming her.

Anxiety can grip people and make them helpless to move, even when they can see little reason for it. Holly was bright and bubbly and had a fun personality, but when the anxiety took hold, she really struggled to control it. From a seed of an idea as a child, unchecked, Holly's anxiety had become all-consuming to the point that she could no longer function in day-to-day life. Sadly, this is not an isolated story as many people find themselves trapped by anxiety following incidents within which they felt out of control. Being out of control once can lead to a strong belief that it will happen again, and this provides the perfect environment for increasing levels of anxiety.

Anger

One of the most commonly misunderstood emotions is anger. As with anxiety, this can be linked with a sense of being unable to control one's situation and can stem from past incidents. We saw earlier how abuse can create a sense of guilt or shame for the abused, but it can also lead to anger, totally justified anger, but which doesn't always have an opportunity to come out at the scene of the event itself. This leads to pent-up frustration which can bubble deep within and come to the surface, often at unexpected moments. This is a bit like the 'crying over spilt milk' scenario when someone loses their cool over something quite small, having handled much worse previously.

Many people have an unrecognised anger within at some injustice in their earlier lives, and can get upset, out of all proportion, to a current situation in some cases, without really understanding why they are feeling this way. This is different from the anger alluded to earlier, whereby people are angry and loud deliberately to keep people at a distance. This anger is at the unfairness of what happened to them and anger at the perpetrator of whatever situation they found themselves in. That could be as extreme as the person who raped them, who they dared not get angry with at the time, but who escaped justice. It could be less dramatic, such as a parent who never met their needs, perhaps made worse because they were seen to meet the needs of others.

This unrecognised anger can be fairly harmless at times and go unnoticed, but in times of stress or another unpleasant situation, or maybe when someone feels threatened or out of control, it will add to the emotion of the moment, causing an eruption. The anger of the present day will be reinforced by unresolved past anger and the person may feel powerless to stop themselves displaying it, either with words or physical violence. When unresolved anger is added to today's anger the emotion can be so strong and uncontrollable that it even scares the person themselves when they are angry. Some people may feel angry all the time but not understand where the anger is coming from. Many day-to-day situations will make them short tempered and grumpy, and they become isolated because people decide to keep out of their way. This isolation can make things worse as it reinforces some of the bad feelings they already have about themselves and no one will get close enough to help them recognise and overcome this issue.

In some people, unrecognised anger will show differently because it has become internalised. These people do not erupt in anger; rather they seethe quietly when cross. This is much harder to detect to begin with because there does not appear to be a problem at all. These people seem, on the surface at least, to have dealt well with whatever negative event happened to them. The problem with this approach may come to light when mysterious illnesses appear to be frequent and hard to pinpoint. Fatigue and unexplained pains, abdominal issues or headaches, deteriorating mental health and many other ailments can be triggered by the stress of internalised anger.

Both explosive anger and internalised anger can trigger other strong emotions like resentment and jealousy, which can create a pressure cooker of negative emotions. These can build up and result in the person feeling so overwhelmed that it triggers violent coping mechanisms, or they find themselves in a crisis that they cannot manage by themselves.

Mood swings

While unresolved, unrecognised anger is difficult to live with, mood swings add another dimension. Memories of things that have happened in the past can trigger great sadness or joy, sometimes in close succession. Those coping with mood swings will tell you it's exhausting to be really happy one minute and down the next; add in the raging temper and the day can get really tricky.

Sometimes memories can be triggered by something overt like smells or songs, yet at other times the mood can change suddenly but it's hard to detect why. In these instances it may be a subconscious memory, remembered at a deep level but long since hidden away by the mind because it causes too much pain.

If someone felt they missed out on something like good parenting, seeing another child being cared for well by a parent could trigger a sense of sadness at never having had this experience, almost a grieving pain that the opportunity to receive this has been lost. In adulthood a marriage breakdown can precipitate the same sense of loss for, say, the future that had been planned as a couple within the marriage but is now lost. This can be heightened when another couple are seen to still be together and happy, even if the sadness is not recognised as a direct result of seeing this; the emotion will still be there and so a sudden down swing in mood may occur.

Unpredictable mood swings can make life difficult, especially when their source is not recognised or understood.

SALLY

Sally, who we talked about earlier, faced abuse at home, which left her feeling rejected and alone even within her own home, the memory of which she worked hard to bury.

Before she took the big decision to move out, she had tried to find the acceptance she craved somewhere else and had turned to a group of friends. Her deep need to belong meant that she allowed herself to be used by them so that she found herself in another abusive situation. Her desire to fit in gave them the leverage to get her to accept sexual abuse from members of the group over quite a long period of time before she could take no more. Ashamed, she never discussed this with anyone, feeling that she had brought it upon herself.

There were more memories, buried deep within, but although she tried to contain them, the emotions that came with them spilled out and showed as bursts of anger or extreme mood swings. Sally could be very loud, the joker, screaming with laughter one minute, but angry or tearful for no apparent reason the next. She had never had the opportunity to learn to deal with her emotions around the things that had happened to her, and neither did she really understand any of the emotions she felt or how to control them. She also suffered from long periods of depression and anxiety, was diagnosed with borderline personality disorder

(BPD), and ended up living alone with few friends and suffering from isolation. During this period in her life she attempted suicide many times using different methods including overdosing and trying to hang herself. Fortunately, she never quite succeeded.

Nightmares and PTSD flashbacks

Nightmares come in many guises, often disconnected with what has happened in our daily lives. They play out random stories, for example flying and then crashing to the ground suddenly, which often makes it hard to understand their origin and how to assign any meaning. In extreme situations, though, it seems that they are often more defined. If someone has suffered severe trauma or abuse it's likely that their nightmares will be a reliving of these events. This can be traumatic as it might happen frequently and it's as if the trauma is happening again every night, which can cause real emotional issues.

Bedtime can become a frightening time because there's no way of telling if the nightmare will occur that night, although there is usually an increased expectation that it will, which creates stress and tension in advance. Sometimes the stress itself will be the very thing that precipitates the nightmare, creating a self-fulfilling prophecy. As time goes on there will be a desire to stay awake to avoid the fear of the nightmare or, in extreme cases, night terrors. This will lead to exhaustion and more stress, creating an even more likely environment for the nightmare to occur. This self-perpetuating cycle can go on unchecked for long periods without the right support and help, possibly leading to health problems in the longer term.

LISA

Bedtime was difficult for Lisa; she suffered extreme nightmares within which she was being chased and trapped by a dark figure whose face she didn't see. It was linked to the abuse she had suffered in her adoptive home, but she found it hard to talk about at first, which meant she carried the fear of bedtime alone to begin with.

Getting worked up before bed about what might happen in her dreams meant that sleep was unlikely to occur, which, while it exhausted her, made her feel safer. Unfortunately, it also meant that when she did finally drift off, her sleep was more fitful and disturbed, which was the time the bad dreams came.

It was a difficult cycle she was now in, which needed breaking so that she could both learn how to prepare herself mentally for a good night's sleep and handle the emotions that came with the nightmares if they occurred, too.

Another outworking of the past can be post-traumatic stress disorder (PTSD) flashbacks. These are almost like waking nightmares in that you can suddenly be reliving a past traumatic event. During the original trauma, your brain may have been in fight, flight or freeze mode. 'Should I try to run away, should I stay and fight it out, or should I keep still and play dead?' There wasn't enough time to process the event or your brain didn't want to process it at that time because it was too hard. This meant that you didn't 'file' the memory appropriately in your mind.

As this memory didn't get processed properly, when you get a trigger – a smell, tune, sentence, situation or any combination of these or another linked occurrence – you will suffer a flashback. The brain tries to process the information, but all the distress of the original event is present once again in this moment, which can be overwhelming.

For some people, this can happen even in the absence of some recognisable trigger, although fortunately this does not appear to be common. Like recurring nightmares, this can be really stressful, because the trauma or abuse is relived over and over again. Unlike the nightmare scenario, there is no ability to control it by just not going to sleep, which leaves the sufferer at the mercy of this particular condition. It is frightening to think that in any given situation or moment in time you might suffer a PTSD flashback, which may make you feel removed from reality and out of control of your actions. This puts you in an ongoing state of high alert, which is stressful and exhausting. This is even more distressing if there was a lack of personal control involved in the initial traumatic event, as not having full control is continuing to have an impact on daily living.

Summary

In this chapter we have looked at how events from our lives may have left us feeling. We have seen how our upbringing or losses can leave us with a sense of rejection or low self-worth. We know that abuse can scar us mentally so that we carry anger either internally, punishing ourselves, or externally, as it spills over uncontrollably. We have considered how abuse can also leave us with a sense of guilt or shame, despite it not having been our fault. This and other things from our past can create a deep fear and anxiety that can impact every moment of our lives. We can be left in a constant, tiring state of high alert which can lead to mood swings and nightmares. In some instances we can feel out of control and struggle to cope with daily living.

'Do not grieve, for the joy of the Lord is your strength.'
— Nehemiah 8:10

STEP UP actions

Spend time with God

Now is a good moment to spend some time with God. To do this, find a quiet space with no distractions and ask Him to bring to mind what He wants you to consider.

Think about what you've just read

Consider what we have covered here and perhaps things that you know impacted you, but which we haven't covered in this chapter.

Explore the relevance to you

Write down anything that you believe still impacts you. List both the negative and those positive things that have helped you to become who you are today.

Pray about it

Let's pray for God to prepare your heart to work to overcome any negative effects of these events. You can use the prayer below to get started or pray in your usual way to God, whichever feels most comfortable to you.

Father God, we know that You gave us our feelings and that these should be good because everything that comes from You is good. I know that how I feel right now is not from You, so I pray that You would be with me as I consider where my negative feelings have come from. Protect my heart, Lord, and give me strength as I move forward. Thank you, Lord. Amen.

Uncover scriptures that speak to you

Write scriptures on Post-it notes or coloured card and put them all around the house or in your pocket to support your journey.

Personal journal

Write about the outcomes in your personal journal to remind you just how far you've come on the days when you need encouragement.

3
What Do Other People See?

For many, what other people think of us is incredibly important, even when we say it isn't. No one likes to admit it, but we are influenced in many of our decision-making processes by what we think other people will think of our actions. In fact, I'd go so far as to say that overall we think we are who we think other people think we are. I nearly used this as the title of the book as I'm so convinced it is the truth for many people. Read it slowly – I know it's a bit tricky – but just think about it for a moment.

When you buy a coat, say, after the key things like fit and colour, what do you consider next? Does someone, or several 'someones', come to mind? Do you think 'This'll show them', or do you go back for the black one because it's safe and you won't get any sarcastic comments about it? Or do you get the black one because everyone says black is slimming? When you're trying it on, do you hear negative comments from your past about how you carry yourself and does this influence your choice, or that someone once said black looks good on you? Even when we're not actively thinking about it, other people can influence our choices.

In some homes people grow up thinking that it's right not to talk about their emotions. This may lead to them continuing to live this way their whole lives, either assuming it's wrong to live any other way or just unable to talk about how they feel. This can create conflicting emotions internally if someone's natural instinct is in opposition to the general family responses. This can be tiring and stressful if it continues long term and people may not realise the negative impacts this can have on them.

LYN

In Lyn's family home she felt that problems were never discussed. Many hints were given about how people were feeling, which created a tense atmosphere sometimes, but no one ever told the others outright what they thought. It appeared to her that the consequence of this was that the parents carried on falling out silently. They would not speak directly to each other for days, or talk about only superficial things, but never the main issue. For the children this was difficult to understand. As they grew older, they recognised how the game worked and started to communicate in the same way.

When Lyn first arrived at Karis, she was so quiet it was easy for people to forget she was even there. She would watch everything going on but rarely ventured an opinion; when she did she would apologise for it moments later. Just having an opinion was deemed unacceptable in her mind.

It transpired that while the adults did not argue or criticise one another openly, the mother was quick to pick on Lyn. It seemed that her mother's frustration at not being able to speak out in general was taken out on Lyn and what her mother perceived as her many shortcomings. She was told she was not as clever or as pretty as her sister and cousins, being told frequently that she was the odd one out, the ugly duckling. Whatever clothes she wore, her mother would criticise and continually belittle Lyn who, once she was old enough, left home immediately. This added more fuel to the mother's fire as here, in her opinion, was visible confirmation of Lyn's stupidity. In this situation it's highly likely that Lyn's mother had some previous negative experience that had impacted her. People talk about 'hurt people hurting people' and this was a clear example. When someone suffers from low self-worth they may attempt to elevate themselves by putting another down.

Trust

Sometimes worrying what others think goes a step further and people find it hard to trust others. There is a fear that trusting others will lead to a breaking of confidence, that the person they've trusted will share widely what secrets they have discovered. No amount of encouragement and support works quickly in this situation, but often staying consistent over a period of time helps the trust to grow, albeit slowly. This is often an illogical fear at face value, based on someone's previous relationships, in which they have been repeatedly let down after sharing openly, but they inwardly expect all relationships after that encounter to be the same. This notion can result in someone feeling trapped by a situation, but powerless to do anything about it, as they are afraid of another breach of trust. Trust is a fragile commodity; it takes a long time to build, but it can be shattered almost instantly with inappropriate words or actions.

Without doubt trust is important in all relationships and, when people have grown up in situations where this has not been recognised, this can cause problems during current day-to-day relationships. This can be particularly difficult in a therapeutic relationship, as almost all therapy depends on trust as a vehicle to disclosure, which is the pathway to discovery and recovery, but without trust the first step on the journey cannot be taken. In some people the reason for the lack of trust is obvious to them, but in others the root cause is not known and so more difficult to resolve. If you know your parents made repeated promises but did not stick to them, or friends in school shared with others something you told them in confidence, or you discovered your husband had had affairs behind your back, it's plain to see that you might have trust issues. The mind, however, is good at protecting us and may have hidden these or other disappointments deep in the subconscious, so we don't know why we find it hard to trust.

One of the problems with not trusting people is that it's hard to tell anyone about how you are feeling. This lack of connection with others can leave you isolated, which carries plenty of problems in itself, but it may also have you feeling like you're the only one this has ever happened to. This makes you even more isolated; there's no way of finding out if you're the only one struggling if you can't explain that you are struggling to anyone. This brings about feelings of inadequacy and hopelessness, a growing belief that you can never be well and that something must be wrong with you, as everyone else appears to be just fine.

Sadly, there are some who will seek out people in this position and work hard to befriend them and become the only person they will trust. This can have terrible consequences as the evil befriender will manipulate and use the isolation created to control the other person totally, for their own gain. It quickly becomes a situation whereby the inability to trust others can leave someone trapped in this kind of negative relationship indefinitely. They are still more afraid of trusting other people than the person who has befriended them. There can also be times when they are actually too terrified of what the befriender will think if they decide to talk to others about their circumstances.

___

LYN

Unfortunately, due to her mother's consistent undermining and belittling of her, Lyn fell into another negative relationship with a friend who treated her the same as her mother did. Lyn had by now come to believe all her mother's unkind words, and, because her father had never spoken out against his wife regarding Lyn, she assumed he felt the same way about her. She had gone from one negative relationship with her mother into another similarly negative and controlling relationship with her friend. This made her feel really bad about herself, trapped and out of control, yet unable to speak up for herself because speaking out was not what she saw growing up. She actually believed it was wrong to say 'Hold on, I'm not happy in this situation', and so stayed unhappily trapped there for several years.

By the time she came to us she was convinced it was not OK to have an opinion and would not make even the smallest decision in case she got it wrong and upset someone. She made us chuckle because she would come in and say she had been really ratty with everyone because she was so cross and felt sure she should apologise, when in fact her tiny annoyance had been almost undetectable to most of us. It was a step forward for her to let us know she had an opinion, albeit unnoticeable. Before that she wouldn't dare to express it at all, or would come and tell us about it in case someone thought badly of her, so she spent much of her day apologising for everything.

In other cases the perpetrator of whatever traumatic deed began this cycle may have talked in terms of 'this is our little secret, never share it with anyone'. Both adults and children have been trapped by this one for differing reasons. Firstly, this creates a bond; secrets are usually special, you are lucky if someone wants to share their secrets with you. This makes the person feel chosen and valued. Secondly, there is often an implied threat behind 'this is our secret', sometimes veiled but at other times overt. This may be accompanied by hints about what might be done to the person or their family if they share the little secret with anyone. However bad, the secret is kept for fear of reprisals. When you work with someone who has this kind of threat-based secret it is incredibly difficult to break into it to get the truth. It's almost like a minor form of programming of the mind and will to perform as desired. Even many years later, victims are often determined to 'keep the secret' despite its known and ongoing harmful nature. Often the fear of the now absent perpetrator is still the strong and driving factor.

Unlovable

Worrying about what others think of us also links to our need to know whether anyone will ever care about us. Will anyone stick by us even when we get it wrong? Are we lovable? One of the deepest concerns is often linked to our parents – if my mother didn't love me, who could? Doesn't that make me unlovable? If my parents, who created me, don't see any good in me, why would anyone else? It's a plaintive cry but found in the hearts of a surprising number of people when you get to talk more with them – the belief that 'nothing I ever did was good enough', or 'my dad wanted only boys, so he ignored me'. 'He was only interested in my grades... my brother... his favourite child...' or any number of other statements along similar lines are spoken and believed every day.

It doesn't stop in childhood, either. The wife whose husband leaves her for a younger woman worries whether anyone else will love her now she's older, since he apparently went searching for youth. She may feel worthless and discarded and wonder if anyone will stick by her if he didn't after they'd been married for many years and had children together. It seems that when someone close to us doesn't see or respond to us as we think they should it changes how we see ourselves, sometimes quite dramatically and often permanently.

While more often it is the impact of someone close that can change or create our own view of ourselves, a stranger has the power to do it too. In a situation where someone is sexually abused or raped, for example, afterwards the victim may now see themselves differently, perhaps as dirty or used. Their previous understanding of who they were and their ability to be cared for and loved may come into question in their mind, not just immediately after the event but for a long time. They may feel unlovable and think that no one will want to be with them now. In fact, they may feel that they cannot be with anyone else because the memory of how the rapist saw them and behaved towards them will always be on their mind.

The issue of whether even God will still love them may come into question. They may even begin to wonder if God ever loved them – if He did, why did He let this happen? It may be too hard at this point to consider that God would have been there and protected them from a much worse outcome. This understanding will come, but much later in the healing journey.

Most people, despite struggling to trust, still have a deep desire to be known. People will do many and varied things to avoid telling others about themselves when they struggle with trust, but in reality they still have a need for someone to know them well. This is why, even though it is the natural order of things, people struggle when both their parents die. There is no one left who knows all about them, good or bad, no one knows all their history, the little things they got up to as kids, how they passed through the transitional steps of life – who they were and who they've become. There is no one left to remember what a brave boy or girl they were when they broke their arm, that their left eye twitches when they're fibbing (probably handy not having someone knowing about that). We all need to be known. It makes us feel safe. We need someone to 'get us' because it makes us feel valued.

SUSIE

Susie, who I introduced earlier, lost both her parents in her late teens after having moved into a foster home as a child. She struggled a great deal with trust. She told none of the other girls in the house any of her story; while we don't encourage over-sharing, they usually share little bits about their lives with one another. She didn't discuss anything with staff, either, and it took a really long time in our one-to-one meetings before she began to unwrap her past – what had happened and how she felt about it.

As she talked about some of the relationships she had tried to form subsequently, before coming to us, it transpired that they were often built around a fantasy in her head of who these people could become to her, rather than actual existing relationships. She targeted a teacher who was kind to her and built this teacher up in her head to be almost perfect, on a pedestal, even. Despite her lack of trust normally, Susie told this teacher everything about herself and found out all she could about her. She was attempting to know and be known in this relationship.

Unfortunately, the teacher didn't recognise what was happening and did not put appropriate boundaries in place in time. Eventually, Susie had to move schools because the teacher accused her of stalking. Susie was distraught as she had invested a lot of time and trust into this relationship without understanding how real relationships actually work. Unfortunately, no one around her understood what was happening, either.

She withdrew from those around her further and the whole situation became one more step into isolation for the child in Susie who, despite her lack of trust, was desperate to make a connection, to be known, to find someone who would truly 'get her'.

Relationships

When we meet people who seem to understand us quickly, we want to know them more. What they think of us becomes important because they seem to understand us without lengthy explanation. That makes us feel okay, normal(ish), accepted. We return the favour by showing that we know them, and a friendship begins to form. In two emotionally healthy people this usually grows well as they spend time together and share mutually enjoyable experiences. The relationship deepens and becomes more dependable and finds a level which is acceptable to both parties – either still a little superficial because of time constraints, or maybe it becomes a deep and lasting friendship. A relationship where there is mutual trust, respect and love, a place of safety, somewhere each person feels 'known' and valued. They 'get' one another.

It all sounds so simple that you wonder why it can be such a difficult path to take. The secret in that scenario was the two 'emotionally stable people'. Unfortunately, so many people are not emotionally stable it's hard to imagine how we create any healthy relationships. By emotionally stable I mean people who have an ability to remain constant and balanced in most situations, who have learned how to handle their emotions and continue to work on that rather than giving in to their failings or disappointments. When relationships in the past were difficult or unusual in the way they functioned, we take a little of each of those with us into new relationships. That can make life awkward, because these are not those old relationships. We talked earlier about how trusting can be hard for those who have been let down in the past, as the feelings generated originally stay with us; this can have a similar effect while trying to build relationships.

If a previous relationship was controlling we fear that the next one might be, and it's true that sometimes people have a tendency to seek out similar people to past partners or even parents, which could account for why this happens repeatedly for some people. Obviously if someone has come out of a bad relationship they don't deliberately look to get themselves back into a similar position, but it takes a degree of self-awareness to recognise that might be your pattern before you can begin to correct that behaviour.

It may be that as a child someone never managed to please a parent and subconsciously looks for a relationship with someone else who responds to them in the same way that parent did, hoping in some way to fulfil the desperate need to please the parent. That can't happen because this is a different person, but the striving to please the person in the new relationship can create an imbalance. The last partner may have been violent and demanding; this can also make a person work hard to please a new partner before the violence starts in this relationship, too, also creating an imbalance.

Most poor past relationships create an emotional insecurity which, alongside trying to please someone else, can also help to form a dependency and in some cases almost an addiction as there is a real need to be with that person all the time, to the exclusion of all others. This eventually destroys the relationship, either because the other person feels smothered or because extreme jealousy creeps in and neither party can find a way to deal with the impact of this. When the insecurity is extreme, how the other person feels about the dependent party is crucial – it's almost like their life blood. A negative response can send them into an emotional downward spiral, while just a few kind and supportive words can leave them ecstatic. They may spend the time away from the other person planning ways to be back with them again sooner than would normally occur.

Belonging

Insecurity isn't just found within a one-on-one relationship; it can permeate all relationships around us. We can feel that others have more rights than us, so we keep quiet in case someone notices we don't belong there, or we get loud and call everyone's bluff, pretending that we're confident and have as much right as anyone else to be there. Which we have, of course, but we don't quite believe it because of our insecurity. People say knowledge is power, so in our insecurity we seek knowledge, believing it will make us powerful so people will want us there. We hang out with the powerful people, hoping that in itself will make us appear powerful, even though we still don't believe we have any right to be there.

The tiny bits of information gleaned from the perceived 'important people' will be used to show just how valuable the important people think we are as they trust us with information. We then pretend we know more by sharing small bits of information with a knowing smile or a 'I couldn't possibly say what I know' (which is next to nothing, but so what). These snippets can also be added to, when no one else can check the facts, again implying that we are important by association.

Lying openly to others may not be a problem for someone with extreme insecurity; they will take the risk of being found out rather than allowing themselves to be seen as weak. How they think other people see them is crucial to their functioning; the smoke and mirrors are essential to avoid anyone realising just how insecure they really are. Other insecure people are more likely to spot them, which makes them instant enemies, not allies as you might expect. This may be due to the fact that we tend to hate most in others what we dislike most in ourselves – who wants to be thought of by others as insecure? It could also be because of a fear of them having power over us with this knowledge. It's ironic that it often doesn't occur to us that they may be thinking just the same about us.

The desire to be known is another area where what we know can be stretched to make others think differently about us. Being known is only part of the story; having somewhere we belong is the rest. Belonging is really important for many people, especially if the family home was not warm or supportive or someone didn't feel part of even their own family. The desire to be accepted and to belong within a family is deep in most people. In searching for a family, similar behaviour to the above can occur. If someone makes us welcome in their home as a relationship is growing, we begin making out to others that we are there more than we really are, or that we know more about their home than we really do. We may talk as if we're often all over the house when in reality we've never left the lounge. This implies that we are accepted there; maybe others around us will think better of us, maybe others will also accept us more readily as a result of us now belonging to a family.

As time progresses, we become useful. Putting on the kettle and making the tea, washing up after a meal; these are day-to-day jobs one doesn't usually do as a guest in someone else's home, as these are only done by the family. Does that make us one of the family? Of course not, but for the person who needs to belong, when they are spoken of as 'like one of the family' or 'part of the furniture', that's exactly what they've been working towards. They have been waiting to be seen by the family as one of them, belonging. They're desperate for others to see them that way, too. In extreme situations there may even be a change of name by deed poll to prove their allegiance and that they fit in. Usually, none of this behaviour is deliberate; it is a pattern the person has fallen into as they handle their insecurity and deep need to belong. Having others tell them they belong is the ultimate aim. Unfortunately, sooner or later they realise that this is not real and usually only a temporary situation, or something changes in the family dynamic which pushes them out. This leaves them more troubled even than before because this is now another failed attempt at building relationships, at finding a family where they can belong.

LISA

Following her abuse in her adoptive family home, Lisa struggled with a sense that she didn't belong anywhere.

Her birth mother had abandoned her and her adoptive family had not defended her when she was being abused within the home. She needed to be accepted as part of a family, any family.

Her desire to belong was so deep that anyone who showed her the slightest interest would get Lisa's full attention. No matter what was expected from her in return she would fulfil the role of perfect daughter, doing whatever was required to become useful and part of the family. She also went as far as changing her name to the family name of a friend after this family made her feel as if she belonged there. Unfortunately, this led to another abusive situation and once again she found herself being used and unable to escape.

She was eventually able to disclose her situation to a church leader who stepped in and supported her to come to Karis.

Comparison

Another way that we worry about how other people see us is comparison. When we stop seeing ourselves for who we are, we start comparing where we fit among others in our world. This is a recipe for disaster either way. If we look at people and believe we are better or more important than them, we may see them in a negative light. We might ignore them or choose to exclude them from the group or activities we are involved in because they do not live up to our expectations; in some cases they make us feel better about ourselves as we feel superior to them. Some may even seek to put those people down in the hopes of gaining greater personal popularity. It's been repeated many times since Theodore Roosevelt apparently first said it: comparison is the thief of joy. When we judge ourselves alongside others, we will rarely be content, yet our achievements are still our achievements, no matter what others achieve.

We call it the comparison trap at Karis because it traps people into such negative thought processes. There is literally nothing helpful about comparing ourselves with others, yet we all do it. When we walk into an event, say, we check the room to see where we fit. Are we dressed correctly according to the majority? We may have felt great when we finished getting ready to go out at home, but now we look around the room and feel underdressed. We wish we had added that scarf, belt, bag or whatever – why? We didn't think we needed it when we got dressed at home, so why would we need it now? The answer is firmly in the fact that we are not looking at just ourselves anymore; we are comparing ourselves with everyone else in the room and suddenly we're not enough. More than that, we think that's what they are thinking about us too – that we're not enough. Guess what? In many cases they are thinking the same about themselves, not judging us at all. That's the problem with the comparison trap: no one wins.

Our girls at Karis often get hung up on believing that other girls are getting more attention than they are, or that someone else is moving on more quickly than them, and it can have devastating effects on their own progress. They all have one-to-one time with senior staff members to work through their issues from the past, but when they start comparing themselves with others in the house they lose track completely. They become so hung up on the comparison that they take up time in multiple one-to-one sessions grumbling about the unfairness of it all instead of focusing on what they are there for. Even when we try to redirect them, they just can't seem to let it go. It becomes their complete focus of attention and it is incredibly difficult to get them to see that they are themselves, not the other person, and what the other person thinks or is doing, or what we're doing in response, is not their business. Neither does it need to have an impact on them unless they choose to allow it to. They become especially obsessed if they think the other person is getting away with something they are not, or getting something they don't deserve, even if they themselves don't want it. It is strange how difficult they find it to stop obsessing about what they think the other person thinks about it. Often this becomes a kind of groupthink situation. One girl decides that another is getting treatment deemed unfair to everyone else and so sets about getting the other girls to think the same. Once she has them all onside, thinking like her, it appears to validate her belief that she must be right. Convincing them that comparison is unhelpful at best takes a long time. Meanwhile they are stagnant, not progressing with their recovery, because comparison with someone else is deemed, in that moment, much more important to them.

Many people get caught up in caring too much about what others have or are getting away with, sometimes to the detriment of their progress. It's much easier to focus on what someone else has than to work for things yourself. It's also easier to get hung up on what you perceive others are doing wrong without them being held to account than it is to identify and work through your own shortcomings. It's surprising, when we start to break it down, just how what other people think about us and what we think about them can impact our lives and influence our decision-making processes, even when we don't think we are affected by it. What we should be more concerned with, in reality, is what God thinks of us, and there's plenty of evidence for that.

Summary

In this chapter we have looked at how other people might affect us. We've considered how other people's responses to us can leave us feeling. A difficulty trusting others can have developed, triggered by how we've been treated in the past. It can lead to a fear of never being good enough for anyone to love us. This makes it hard to build good relationships and leaves us feeling like we don't belong anywhere. Insecurity from this can make us compare ourselves with others in an unhealthy way. Many and varied things from our past work away quietly in the background to cause us all kinds of problems in this area, often without us having been aware – until now.

'Am I now trying to win the approval of human beings, or of God? Or am I trying to please people? If I were still trying to please people, I would not be a servant of Christ.'
— Galatians 1:10

STEP UP actions

Spend time with God

Now is a good moment to spend some time with God. To do this, find a quiet space with no distractions and ask Him to bring to mind what He wants you to consider.

Think about what you've just read

Consider what we have covered here and how other people may have impacted your life and perhaps affected your ability to trust.

Explore the relevance to you

Write down any of the situations you've just read that you recognise from your life. Identify, where you can, what you think may have triggered them.

Pray about it

Let's pray for God to open the eyes of your heart to understand what created the emotions you feel. You can use the prayer below to get started or pray in your usual way to God, whichever feels most comfortable to you.

Father God, we know that You love us even when we don't feel it. I pray You would be here with me as I consider when I began to feel unlovable and that I didn't belong. Please help me to see that this simply isn't true as I am loved by You and belong in Your family, always. Thank you, Lord. Amen.

Uncover scriptures that speak to you

Write scriptures on Post-it notes or coloured card and put them all around the house or in your pocket to support your journey.

Personal journal

Write about the outcomes in your personal journal to remind you just how far you've come on the days when you need encouragement.

PART TWO
DISCOVER HOW YOU MANAGE

Part One has started your healing journey by identifying the many things that can impact our lives negatively, whether we are aware of them or not.

In Part Two we will discover the strategies we have developed to help us cope. Some of the ways we manage are quite ingenious and may remain useful. This section of the book will help you to discover which you use and whether these are good for you or not. Identifying these and dealing with them, if necessary, in the STEP UP sections will prepare you for Part Three, where you will begin to recover the real you.

4
How Do I Cope?

Coping mechanisms or strategies are ways we develop over time to help us deal with what comes at us day to day. They are a way of behaving that enables us to function, whatever has gone wrong in our life. Some of them will be brief and get us over a major crisis, while others will become long-standing. This is to protect us from the same bad thing happening to us again or to help us forget that it ever happened. Some coping mechanisms are helpful, indeed essential, to our day-to-day living. Others can be incredibly negative and, instead of keeping us safe, they can alienate us from those around us and leave us isolated.

While we are aware of some of our coping mechanisms, many of them come from our subconscious without us actively doing anything to make them occur. They are patterns of behaviour that establish and adapt to our situations over time until they are unrecognisable from how they started out. This is why it can be so difficult to unravel this behaviour pattern in attempting to create a change for the better. Sometimes these behaviours have become more destructive to the person than the original event or events they were constructed to handle in the first place. This makes it imperative that they are dealt with, but finding the source can take a lot of time and patience and occasionally needs an outside eye to help someone navigate their way through it.

Overall, though, we must remember that these strategies have been our method of survival in tough situations. When we become aware of them and handle them appropriately they can have a positive side. Let's have a look at what kinds of behaviours would be considered coping mechanisms.

The mask

One of the better documented and well-known coping strategies is the wearing of a mask. Obviously, this isn't a literal mask, but rather behaving outwardly in a manner that really isn't how you are feeling on the inside. We all do it to some degree in everyday life. Who hasn't smiled when someone we don't like has come towards us, even though on the inside we are thinking 'I really don't want to talk to you'? When we carry on smiling as if everything is fine but we're in so much pain that all we really want to do is sit down with our feet up, this is a kind of temporary mask. This form of temporary mask is totally normal, and everyone does it to a greater or lesser degree; this is normal behaviour, rightly or wrongly. In the past this was often termed 'keeping a stiff upper lip' and as such men in particular can be negatively affected in this area.

The negative side of this coping strategy is when someone cannot show how they are feeling at all, ever. Their world is such an unhappy place, but they just keep going so well that even those closest to them do not realise how bad things are. The reasons for this can be varied. Sometimes people feel that if they let on how bad they are feeling others will judge them or won't want to know them anymore. Their fear of people exiting their world and leaving them alone prevents them from sharing. Unfortunately, this can still leave them isolated because, even with those people continuing to be physically around them, there is no longer a genuine connection as the honesty in the relationship has gone.

Some believe that they need to keep up a front because those around them would not cope if they fell apart or disclosed their true feelings. This again can leave them somewhat isolated unless they are able to share their issues with someone else who is maybe not as close to them, someone who they feel will not be negatively impacted to hear that they are struggling. In reality, coping secretly with unhelpful emotions can backfire when keeping up the pretence becomes too much and the person explodes emotionally, unexpectedly and uncontrollably. The shock of this reaction to the nearest and dearest can cause devastation, particularly if the coping strategy of mask wearing has also covered up other secretive negative coping mechanisms, which may now come to light.

LISA

Before Lisa was taken from her birth mother's home and put into foster care, she was often left alone by her mother to care for her younger siblings. The conditions were appalling, and she was young but she felt she had to hold it together for her siblings. This belief carried on through her foster care placement into her adoptive home, even though she was being abused and was unhappy.

Many years later, when she finally made contact again with her younger sister, the same sense of having to appear okay came into play. For a long time, to protect her sister from how damaged she had become, she gave her the impression that she was over it all and was doing really well. She was so good at this mask that the sister started loading her problems on Lisa too, which she was not yet strong enough to cope with.

The relationship began to slide as the sister couldn't understand why, if she was doing so well, Lisa had to stay where she was and not move nearer to her to help.

Eventually Lisa had to confess that she had not been fully truthful because she was being too protective. She really needed more time to come to terms with her past.

Others just feel so low they cannot speak the words; it's like trying to voice the unspeakable to them. It's as if, so long as they don't talk about it, they can pretend it didn't happen or the sadness they are feeling isn't real. Sometimes it may be that resentment and bitterness towards someone else has become so rampant in their mind that they are afraid to even begin to talk about the subject for fear of being unable to stop, or of the damage they may cause the other person once they start to voice how they feel.

People pleasing

Another sort of wearing a mask is to behave a bit like a chameleon. This animal can reflect different colours by shifting crystals within its cells to make itself blend into its surroundings. Sometimes when people are desperate to fit in, or want to belong, they will alter their behaviours to reflect their surroundings. They hope that this will make them more acceptable to others in this environment. Essentially, this is people-pleasing going too far. There is no harm in doing nice things for other people, but when the primary drive is to be accepted at any cost it is not healthy. Over time they may completely lose sight of their own self as they strive to behave in a manner pleasing to those around them, even if that isn't how they would normally behave, or they don't feel comfortable doing it. It creates again this mismatch between how they are behaving externally and how they are feeling internally, which creates something psychologists call cognitive dissonance. This essentially means an imbalance that is hard to live with long term and creates its own emotional problems on top of those that were already present.[5]

People can be doing this on purpose or be completely unaware until someone else points it out, and even then they may not agree that they are. Either way, it can create issues because of their unconscious struggles in the battle they are essentially having with themselves. It can be tiring to fight with yourself daily, even unwittingly. This people-pleasing can result in further harm due to people over-committing their time to help others. The need to be needed is a way of bolstering self-worth, making it impossible to say no to the demands of others even when it becomes detrimental to our health and wellbeing. It's been said that we are human beings, not human doings, and that we should consider this fact when we begin to over-commit to doing things, for ourselves or for others. There are other schools of thought that what we do stems from our being, which is also true, but more

5   G Davey, *Complete Psychology*, Second Edition (Hodder Education, 2014)

important here is to find the balance between being and doing, which is easier said than done.

Building walls

In trying to protect ourselves from further damage we can become fearful of relationships with others, unable to commit in the ways we did before we felt harmed by someone else's actions. We can put up barriers to communication to keep people at arm's length. Our safe walls that we hide behind are built one brick at a time. Avoiding eye contact with someone – brick, returning a one-word answer to an open question – brick, being aggressive in our body language – brick, and many other bricks are added. Before we know it, we are behind a high wall. It's safe behind that high wall, isn't it? But we can become trapped behind it, so that when we want to reach out for help we no longer can. As a coping strategy it kept us safe, but as time passes we discover that now, instead of safe, in reality we are trapped; our behaviours have become so ingrained that we no longer feel able or know how to call for help or accept it if it is offered. Now our learned behaviours, instead of keeping us safe, can make us truly isolated and helpless. Feigned aggression can become our normal way of responding to others, keeping them at a distance even if we've decided we want a relationship with them. While we might crave relational interaction, we feel unable to trust anyone enough to start this process. The walls we've built to keep us safe have been added to so much over time that we have no idea how to start this process and are still anxious at the risks involved. In this situation we might settle for being around people, but not fully committed. We are afraid of connection, though desiring interaction, so we try hard not to be noticed and blend into the background.

SUSIE

When Susie first joined us at Karis she was like a shadow for many months. She was short, petite, and only ever wore black, including a black woolly hat to cover the fact that in her extreme distress she had chopped all her hair off some weeks before arriving. While she was with the other girls, she rarely spoke or showed any emotion; it was hard to know what she was thinking. Given the chance, she would withdraw to her bedroom, as she barely tolerated the activities she was expected to participate in the rest of the time.

She had built incredibly effective high walls despite a genuine desire to connect and be known. Various life events had confirmed in her mind that people would be taken from her if she allowed them to become important to her, so she kept everyone at arm's length. All her day-to-day behaviours showed us that, despite what she was saying about not wanting to trust anyone, underneath she clearly craved connection. She was so cautious around people, watching, listening, always there, but rarely speaking for fear of being noticed and expected to contribute, which might give away what she was thinking. While we encouraged her, we sensed that she was fragile, like a little sparrow ready to fly away at any moment if the threat level became too great.

Her emotional walls had trapped her firmly behind them, but brick by brick we helped her to start removing them. Unfortunately, we were at an early stage with Karis, and through my desire to help her to freedom I made the mistake of not putting the appropriate boundaries in place. While she began to trust and share some of her history with us, I realised too late that I had now become her focal relationship. Although this was far from ideal, it did mean that she was beginning to open up and to start building relationships with others too, so we decided I just had to accept the situation at this time and be more careful in the future.

While Susie was quite an extreme example, many people can emotionally withdraw even if they've actually managed to get themselves into a group setting. If this is a deliberate ploy to be around people but not committed, like Susie, that's one thing, but if you are in a roomful of people and completely unable to connect, that can be incredibly isolating. To have built such high walls that you simply cannot connect even when you would like to can make you feel totally alone, more so than actually being alone.

Manipulation

Now we've alienated those around us by our self-protective behaviours, forming relationships is pretty tricky. That might seem fine to begin with but eventually there is a desire for a genuine connection with others, not just the superficial ones we have allowed until now. This is where manipulation can sneak in; it can take many forms and recognising if you use any of these is hard. Sometimes the manipulation is genuinely unrecognised by the person doing it because it has become so much part of their way of coping. We have had girls in Karis, and also other people that I have met, who are so expert that it takes a while to spot it. As with many of these things a pattern has begun to emerge so that I become aware of it sooner now. Even so, it is still difficult to determine whether the manipulation is deliberate or if it's a subconscious way of coping following earlier abuse or trauma.

I only have space to mention a couple of manipulations here as there are so many and they are so varied but when you know them you will recognise them again and again. We talked in Chapter One about *how* we became who we are; this can impact the type of manipulation we use as a coping strategy. If, say, we suffered rejection at some point and this really bruised us emotionally, we won't want to risk feeling like that again, so the likelihood is that if we even consider building another relationship, we will make sure that the person doesn't reject us.

How can we achieve this, as people always have that choice? Well, it's generally human nature not to kick a dog when it's down, so if we are perceived as down on our luck it's less likely that someone will feel able to walk away from us. To this end we will, fairly early on in the relationship, give them our tale of woe. What we must remember here is that most people using this form of manipulation are not aware of what they are doing. Depending on where we are in our journey, we may share the sadness from our past or the bad situation we are in today to make them feel sorry for us, hoping this will stop them rejecting us too. This is of course simplified, but if the right person has been selected for this form of manipulation they can soon find themselves providing all sorts of emotional and practical support, particularly if they themselves are not good at boundary setting. The relationship can become all-consuming because those suffering from past rejections rarely know how to build good relationships and can become controlling in a passive-aggressive way. They know how to be quietly demanding, using methods that create feelings of guilt in others and a desire not to hurt the manipulative person more than they've been hurt before. This leads to them getting their own way and a lot of attention, which is their prime aim.

SALLY

Sally quite unwittingly became a master at this. By carefully selecting people with kind hearts she gathered a small group of older women who were concerned by her plight and who between them took good care of her. As is often the case with people as damaged as Sally, she had built walls to protect herself, a coping mechanism we discussed earlier. This made her feel safe enough to ask people to do things for her and enabled her to become a skilled manipulator of people who could tend to her needs, even though she wasn't at that time aware of what she was doing. She no longer sought meaningful relationships with people her own age after her bad experiences previously. Friendships that seemed to her safer were established only with older people who would care for her and give her what she needed. Unfortunately, these kinds of demanding relationships become tiring for the carer, especially if the carer had no idea that this would become their role in the relationship.

Sally would wear people out over time with her demands and they would fall away, particularly if they hadn't been good at setting boundaries early on in the relationship. At some point during this period Sally threw herself off a second-storey balcony in another suicide attempt and fractured her spine. This was now her ace card in all of her needy relationships or if anyone challenged her situation.

Now disabled from her fall, she had acquired disability benefits and a Motability car, and travelled either in a wheelchair or a mobility scooter, walking for only short distances using two sticks. Being officially classed as disabled gave Sally a persona. Without realising it she adopted completely the role of an ill person; it became her whole identity. Her disability defined her. She considered that she was entitled to things because her life was so bad, and she took no responsibility for anything that had happened to her. Having absolutely no insight into her own coping mechanisms, if people didn't respond the way she expected them to when she needed them she would become frustrated and depressed. This would lead to her contacting them, sometimes in the middle of the night, and threatening to kill herself. Some of them fell away at this point, unable to cope anymore, but one kind soul stuck with her and eventually brought her to us.

If maternal deprivation was the key issue in childhood, the desire to replace the missing mother figure will create a much more directed manipulation towards just one person at a time. If you ask most people, they would consider having a loving mother perfectly normal. For some, though, this has not been their experience and, as mentioned earlier, this can have long-lasting repercussions, especially if they too believe having a loving mother should be normal. Their sense of loss at what they never had can be intense. I've heard people describe it as physical pain to see others of their age with their mothers when they haven't had that relationship and can never experience this.

The manipulation begins with careful selection of someone who might fit the bill of the missing or uncaring mother. Obviously always a woman, the person selected will need to be older and appear caring and maternal. The manipulation can actually work both ways; if after a while it is apparent that the 'substitute mother' does not actually fit the previously hoped for mother figure, the expectations can be adapted or the substitute's attributes can be created in the mind of the manipulator. In this situation, bizarrely, both parties are in effect being manipulated, yet in all likelihood neither is aware. The manipulation in this situation is in how the behaviour is carried out rather than the outcome, which the manipulator may not be fully aware of at the outset. Situations will be created to put both parties into a parent/child dynamic wherever possible to mimic a true home life setting. These will become as frequent as the manipulator can manage. They may even result in the use of the term 'mum' or 'mummy' as this provides the much sought-after emotional satisfaction. Unfortunately, the illusion is rarely sustainable, and after a while the next 'mother substitute' will be lined up in readiness for this one failing.

LISA

We looked at Lisa earlier as she attempted to become part of a family, despite finding herself back in another abusive situation. Lisa is desperate for a mother, having been abandoned by her birth mother and so badly let down by her adoptive mother.

She attempted to recreate a mother relationship with the church leader who brought her to us and has tried to create mother/child relationships with myself and other staff at Karis by behaving exactly as described above. It is important that we lovingly maintain boundaries while she works through these situations. We are also explaining to her along the way why this is important for her, so that she fully understands our actions. Without this she may feel rejected again and revert back to this behaviour in the future, but more covertly.

Control

Perhaps one of the most common coping mechanisms is needing to be in control. This can cover a multitude of behaviours required to achieve that sense of controlling your own environment and everything in it. This is one of the strategies that can be seen as positive because it may keep you safe in a dangerous situation.

In all new situations I used to find myself checking escape routes and liked to sit at the end of rows, or on a table near the door with my back to the wall. I would also check out as much as possible about a place I was going to spend time in if I hadn't been there before. I'm sure I'm not the only one, but it doesn't alter the fact that I was actually attempting to have as much control as possible over my environment.

I know why I did this; my first husband was an alcoholic and violent when he'd been drinking. It became second nature to me to identify escape routes to keep myself safe and I hadn't actively changed my thinking since then. When I handed over control of my life to God he healed me of my need to sit on the end, so I can now sit further along a row of seats. Checking for exits is something I still do sometimes, but that's just common sense, isn't it? On a plane they even tell you where they are.

Perfectionism is another of my guilty secrets. I am never satisfied until I've got something absolutely right; although still a work in progress, even this habit is improving. I'm learning to let go and let God take the steering wheel in most situations. People sometimes tend towards perfectionism as a coping mechanism to prevent rejection. They have low self-esteem in many cases but by making sure everything they do is perfect, or as close as they can get it, they hope that they will be accepted for who they are.

This can be part of an obsessive-compulsive disorder (OCD) or simply stand alone. Like the earlier manipulations, it is not always recognised that perfectionism can be used to cover up some perceived personal shortcoming. OCD is an extreme attempt to control every element of personal environment. This is beyond merely a desire to do something well; as the name 'obsessive' suggests, there may be a need to count, clean or maybe line things up in an orderly way which has become out of control – it has become an obsession. Like many of the other coping strategies we've discussed, this is something that has got out of control and now needs dealing with for its own sake. When we insist on this level of control, we're saying we don't trust God to keep us safe.

Disliking sudden or unexpected change is another trigger for those liking to be in control. In fact, it's human nature to kick against change, even planned change. That's why there are so many successful books out there advising on how to move people or organisations through the change process. Change can be scary even if you have a good perspective on life, but if yours is faulty it can create some almost insurmountable difficulties. The coping strategy in this instance is to prepare for every eventuality, often referred to as having 'belt and braces'. There can be an OCD element to this that can cripple people from doing anything in case someone makes changes at the last minute. This can be overwhelming and lead to an inability to cope at all.

Self-harming

When talking about self-harm people tend to think first of things such as cutting, burning, drinking something harmful like bleach, or jumping from somewhere high to cause personal damage. The reasons for this are as varied as the methods used, but the common aim is often to distract from inner pain by creating outer pain. It can also be used as a cry for help when it feels too hard to verbalise a need or extreme emotion. There are additional methods such as starving, bingeing and vomiting. These tend to be more about having control in at least one area of life when other areas may seem too hard or completely out of control.

Self-harm can be a more worrying form of coping because, while it might start quite small with simple scratching or missing a meal, it can become all-consuming and the cutting can become dangerously deep or need to be more and more frequent before it provides the desired emotional release or sense of being in control. Likewise, missing the occasional meal can evolve into a serious eating disorder because of the desire to have something you feel fully in control of.

Most self-harmers will tell you that the action begins as a simple way to cope but often turns into obsessive behaviour over which they have no control. To begin with there is a sense of release at, say, seeing a cut bleed and feeling the pain, both initially and as the wound progresses either to healing or infection. There is often a belief that the pain is deserved because the person is bad in some way. Over time superficial cuts no longer have enough effect and deeper, more painful cutting and more of it is required before the sense of satisfaction is achieved. Unfortunately, the elation from cutting is quickly overridden by the guilt and shame of having given into the urge again. This leaves the cutter in a worse place than before they harmed. This destructive cycle becomes difficult to break out of.

Controlling eating by bingeing and vomiting or by starvation can also take the self-harmer into a destructive cycle after the initial high of being fully in charge of their intake. After a time they can no longer choose whether to eat, binge or vomit but have become trapped within their coping strategy. This is a situation which many do not recognise even when faced with definitive proof.

As with acute physical self-harm, this coping strategy can become life-threatening in itself. Sometimes there is an element of body dysmorphia whereby the person grows to dislike a certain aspect of their body and obsesses over it. It may be that they think they are overweight and so control their food intake excessively, often to a dangerous point. They may add excessive exercising to this, still believing that they are overweight, even when they can see their weight on the scales.

LYN

Lyn found it difficult to express any emotion. She kept her emotions contained but she needed an outlet for them, which came in the form of self-harm. She would cut herself and control her food and fluid intake excessively. If she gave in to bingeing, she would be cross with herself and take back control by vomiting immediately.

She felt she had no control in other areas because she could not express herself. She also believed that she was overweight based on her mother's comments, so needed to use food restriction to give her a sense of being in control. For many years she would vomit after every meal and hardly drank enough to keep her alive. This showed externally in blemishes all over her face and excessively cracked and bleeding lips. Even this external damage, regardless of how underweight she had become, didn't convince her to stop her negative coping behaviours.

Substance misuse

This could reasonably be seen as another form of self-harm. Many people use alcohol to hide their emotional distress. Alcohol is socially acceptable, despite the dangers it holds for the unwary. Almost every big event from birth ('wetting the baby's head') to death (the wake) is celebrated with alcohol. We 'raise a glass' to coming of age, passing exams, going to university, starting a new job, getting married, moving into a new home – the list is endless. Even if we're not celebrating, alcohol still plays its part, as we commiserate alone or with others in our misfortunes. For most people this is okay and doesn't produce lasting damage, but for some it can spiral out of control and lead to addiction. For some, drinking for fun becomes drinking to forget. This takes away choice when sobering up to reality becomes too hard to do, either because the memories are too heavy to carry or because a chemical imbalance has created dependence. The coping mechanism has now become part of the problem and it also needs a solution before it becomes too destructive. Few people recognise this in time, and because of the social acceptability of alcohol it is harder for those around them to notice either. For many it seems that getting drunk on a night out is just normal. Drowning one's sorrows is so expected that identifying someone struggling can be hard. It's a bit like when you're at the seaside: is that person waving or drowning?

There are obviously other forms of substance misuse such as using drugs and, while not as socially acceptable, these can have a tremendous impact on daily living over time, especially if 'recreational' usage has moved into dependency. Most substances are also still illegal, so carry a greater risk. For those with low self-esteem this risk can be regarded as deserved, as they may see themselves as not worth any better. Once again, while early use may have helped in giving temporary respite from bad memories or poor belief systems, as time passes it may become harder to remain in control. Now the coping strategy itself needs coping with.

As we can see, many of our coping mechanisms, while they start out keeping us feeling safe, have the potential to practically take on a life of their own. In some instances, we lose the ability to control the very thing we have introduced into our life to help us cope and we become controlled by it instead. Sometimes we see this spiralling out of control and consider early remedial action, but at other times we are unaware until it's too late. Even when those closest to us identify behaviours that have become dangerous, we cannot or do not take action.

Summary

In this chapter we have looked at how people learn to cope with the impact of their past. We've discovered that there are a lot of potential ways to live and possible coping strategies following trauma, some we don't even know we are doing. We've looked at how people develop many strategies that they believe will keep them safe, some of which are positive. We've also seen how some of these coping mechanisms can in themselves become a danger without people realising before it's too late.

'I am not saying this because I am in need,
for I have learned to be content whatever the
circumstances. I know what it is to be in need,
and I know what it is to have plenty. I have
learned the secret of being content in any and
every situation, whether well fed or hungry,
whether living in plenty or in want. I can do all
this through Him who gives me strength.'
— Philippians 4:11–13

STEP UP actions

Spend time with God

Now is a good moment to spend some time with God. To do this, find a quiet space with no distractions and ask Him to bring to mind what He wants you to consider.

Think about what you've just read

Discover which of the coping strategies we have covered here are similar to strategies you use currently.

Explore the relevance to you

Write down any of the coping behaviours you've just read that you recognise from your life. Where you can, discover what you think may have triggered them. Think about whether they are helping you or causing you harm.

Pray about it

Let's pray for God to reveal to you the coping strategies you use day to day, even the ones that you aren't aware of using. You can use the prayer below to get started or pray in your usual way to God, whichever feels most comfortable to you.

Father God, we know that You are working things out for our good even when we don't see it. I pray You would be here with me as I discover what coping strategies I use and help me to discover what prompted them in my life. Please help me to see which are not helpful to me and remind me that I am not dealing with this alone but that You are here with me. Thank you, Lord. Amen.

Uncover scriptures that speak to you

Write scriptures on Post-it notes or coloured card and put them all around the house or in your pocket to support your journey.

Personal journal

Write about the outcomes in your personal journal to remind you just how far you've come on the days when you need encouragement.

5
What Else Impacts My Thinking?

While we've looked at a lot that can impact how we think, both from our past and in how we cope with that, there can be other factors that impact us. In this chapter it would be helpful to discover what these might be.

Perspective

Everyone sees things from a slightly different perspective. There can be ten people in a room watching a couple having a conversation and everyone will come away with a different viewpoint, even though they all just watched the same conversation play out. Perception is based on many things – upbringing, age, gender, financial status, height and life experiences to name but a few. The list is pretty much endless. With all this said, it's no wonder we sometimes find it really difficult to see things from another's perspective, especially if we struggle with something negative that has happened to us in the past. It can be difficult accepting that not all men are evil if you have been the victim of an evil man. A natural fear may surface around men, even if logic tells you this is unreasonable.

Sometimes when there is disagreement between the girls at Karis and I'm trying to get them to see it from each other's point of view I will hold up my phone and ask them to describe precisely what they are looking at. They will tell me they can see two pink and purple dinosaurs and some stars on a silver background (my granddaughter stuck them on my phone cover). I then describe what I can see – a black rectangle with a white border – then pause and ask them if we are looking at the same thing. Obviously, they say yes, and I use this to illustrate that neither is wrong. We are just looking at it from a different angle, which gives a different perspective, and this is sometimes what happens in life. Neither person is wrong, but each brings their own unique perspective to every situation. 'Instead of looking at life through rose-tinted glasses we look at it through –' and here I get each of them to put their own name in, so for me it would be 'Jenny-tinted glasses'. Try putting your name in there when you need to remind yourself that someone else isn't necessarily wrong; they may just have a different perspective.

If we did not experience love or appreciation in our childhood home, or at least not in a way that was meaningful to us, our perception may be that we must be unlovable. We don't expect love from anyone. If it is offered, we struggle to accept, not believing this is possible for us or assuming that it must be a trick, and we may look for the ulterior motive. After any negative experiences it is common to find it difficult to trust people again. Without exception, all of our young women at Karis found it hard to trust anyone when they first arrived. Trust takes a long time to build and is hard to win, but it is essential to building good relationships with people at every level, especially in the therapeutic setting. Without trust we cannot share even basic things, let alone our deepest secrets, for fear of someone using them against us.

When we see something differently, we may feel others are not being truthful with us. We assume they are deliberately being difficult, because that has been our past experience. This can lead to distrust and increased isolation, especially as our default position may be to assume that everyone is 'out to get us' because it's a 'dog eat dog' world. In reality, someone may genuinely be trying to help us, but we miss out rather than take the risk.

Interestingly, I have a friend who believes that everyone is out to do her good, until they prove otherwise. I, on the other hand, have always believed that everyone is out to do me harm, until they prove otherwise.

Before we had that conversation, it never occurred to me that it could be that way. Now I try to take that into consideration when I meet people. Choosing to do that has allowed me to change my perception of others in a positive way, which usually results in a better outcome.

Attitude

Our attitude can make or break us. Simple. There's little more to say on this, but I will elaborate. There may be a few people hopping mad when I finish this paragraph, but stick with me. Today's world seems to have created a sense of entitlement, not just in one generation; this attitude can arise across the board. The most unfortunate thing about a well-developed sense of entitlement is that if you don't get what you think you are entitled to then you are going to be unhappy. One of the things most people think they are entitled to is to be happy. Says who? To be honest, it is unrealistic to assume that we should be happy all the time. That would in fact rob us of many good but difficult things. If we got everything we wanted without effort, we would never know the joy of personal achievement. The excitement of looking forward to saving up for something then buying it, or the satisfaction of a job well done. Getting everything we want just because we think we're entitled doesn't seem like a great idea in reality, but there are people stuck in that mindset, which sadly prevents them from enjoying some of the simpler things in life.

SALLY

The last time we talked about Sally she was, without any understanding of what she was doing, displaying that sense of entitlement. 'I'm disabled so you owe me, I suffer so life owes me. I should get help with whatever I want whenever I want because I'm not well.' It was not her finest trait, but it was a total cover-up on her part, although even she did not realise it at that time. She was afraid of being rejected so she made people feel unable to walk away. She almost guilt-tripped them into staying and helping her. Some recognised her fear and the kinder ones did not want to add to her pain by rejecting her further, but her attitude made it difficult to like her at that time. This was sad, because underneath all the bluster was a lovely but scared girl.

She was strong-willed and challenging when she came to Karis. Her deep belief in her entitlement was, to say the least, hard to manage, but she believed it was necessary. She was demanding and rude to other students and staff alike if she didn't get her own way. She was hierarchical and treated some of the staff like servants. She would also try to bypass them by withholding her questions and demanding to discuss things with me alone. Fortunately, I am pretty strong-willed myself, but it became a lesson in tightrope walking to keep her from usurping staff while still helping her to move forward. It was tough trying to get her to see things in a different way without upsetting the fine balance of a house full of young women with life-controlling issues. There were some days when I questioned whether I was the person who should be doing this at all. That said, however, she had one enormous redeeming factor: she was willing to listen to your point of view, but it had better be good. You could negotiate with Sally in a way that would encourage her to try to see things differently. It was possible to convince her that if she changed her attitude towards staff they would be supportive, and that it would be to her benefit to work with them and not against them. She was prepared to try to change her attitude and see what happened. Her previous life experiences had been that if she gave people a chance they would reject her, so she had learned not to do that. She asked me once why I thought she had no friends; well, that gave me an open door to talk to her about how our attitude impacts how others respond to us. What a gift of an opportunity to explain, while recognising once again that she had little to no understanding of the impact of her negative coping behaviours.

Being selfish or self-centred is connected to the personal sense of entitlement in that it's an 'I'm owed' mentality. It isn't generally recognised by the person exhibiting the trait – in fact, they usually believe that they only ever do things to help other people. Often people express their main problem as doing too much for others when in fact this is a perception issue. It is true, there may additionally be a payoff for others in their behaviour, but they are usually the biggest winners in any situation. They are careful to ensure it stays that way, even though internally they truly believe their actions are for others. In these situations they will get cross if you challenge them with the truth. If, however, understanding does dawn, they are shocked both at their behaviour and how well they have hidden it even from themselves.

Similar again is the attitude of 'there's not enough'. This attitude can prevail in relationships where self-esteem is an issue. Friendships can become insular, intensely one on one. This 'best friend to the exclusion of all others' scenario is not uncommon in teenage girls, but if the pattern continues repeating into adult-hood it may indicate that one or both parties have issues with self-worth. Allowing other people into the relationship poses a risk to one of them of being replaced. The fear of this and the ensuing jealousy can be devastating. The jealousy is triggered by the usually unfounded belief that the friend cannot pos-sibly have enough love to share with others, that it is limited, so that if they have other friends as well there will not be enough affection or time to go round. It is an irrational fear but very real for the person sensing it. This is especially true if it is rooted in something like a parent or other main carer showing that work was more important than them, or displaying sibling favouritism during childhood.

This attitude can spill over into other areas and show as greed or grabbing. Panic-buying is an obvious outer working of this fear of 'not enough'. Some people feel an inner anger towards others succeeding, which is rooted in the same mentality – the belief that if you do well it's going to be harder for me to do well. This prevents them from celebrating the successes of even those close to them. In their fear and jealousy they miss out on the joy of sharing when others do well.

Another attitude that can impact our thinking is perfectionism. This desire to do everything perfectly is rooted in personal pride, and the deep fear of getting it wrong, of failing in a way that others will see. This is likely rooted in never quite being able to please a parent or carer as a child. Maybe there was some ridicule between siblings when mistakes were made, or punishment was meted out disproportionately to those who got it wrong at home or in school. If a teacher chose to identify and shame pupils for failing in some way, this fear of public shaming may remain in the background and drive the desire to do everything perfectly. While in some instances this can be seen as an advantage, in other situations it can create real problems. Trying to meet tight deadlines at work can be hampered by extreme perfectionism, possibly leading to burn-out in the long term. For some, the fear of failure can mean they never start anything – knowing they cannot afford to make a mistake they would rather not try. In some extreme circumstances, people will find it hard to have an opinion on anything in case it's wrong; something as simple as being offered coffee or tea can seem an unanswerable question.

LYN

This was the case for Lyn when she first came. Having been compared unfavourably with her sister and cousins by her mother, and having all her choices denigrated by her, Lyn felt completely undermined. Going on into another controlling relationship with a friend only confirmed for Lyn that she was incapable of making good decisions.

Her new way of ensuring she didn't fail in her decisions anymore was that she just didn't make them. Having to make a choice put an immense strain on her and she would put up with anything rather than dare to speak out, so ingrained was her fear of failing at decision making. So much so that she couldn't answer you on the spot if you offered her tea or coffee – she would rather go without than commit and get it wrong.

Bullying

While we've touched on this before, it's worth exploring further as it has the potential to impact us negatively, either as the bully or the bullied. Bullying is to do with a lack of self-belief within the bully, who takes out their frustrations, fears and anger on someone they usually perceive as less able than themselves. It's well known that if you are able to stand up to a bully they usually run. Unless, that is, they have surrounded themselves with enough other weak, insecure people to protect them in this instance.

What the bully hasn't realised is that, far from making them look good and their victim stupid, any sensible person will see them for who they are, even if they believe their failings are hidden behind false bravado.

Sometimes, instead of perceiving someone as less able, the bully is intimidated by the person's apparently superior skills. They feel they can never match up, which can trigger jealousy, which may also lead to bullying. In order to feel better about themselves and their behaviour, and safer if challenged by the victim, the bully will convince others around them that their bullying is justified. They will play on other people's insecurities, suggesting somehow that the victim's skills put everyone not as skilled at risk too. This can create fear and stir jealousies, leading to a sort of groupthink where one person becomes ostracised and attacked for being different. This is common in school, workplaces and other enforced groupings but can also surface in friendship groups. It can create a sort of self-protection feeling – if everyone is focusing on one person then the rest of us might be left alone, safe from being picked on.

Bullying can sometimes occur within individual relationships too and be quite hard to manage as it is so undermining. Sometimes we have people in our lives who are just not good for our day-to-day wellbeing. They are not actually against us, but they are so insecure in themselves that they reflect that onto us by their bullying behaviours. When we are with them, we might feel underrated or undervalued to the point that it begins to chip away at our self-esteem. They may not even realise that is what they are doing, and we may not either, but when we are with them, we feel less than our normal selves; we begin to lose our self-worth and feel less capable. We need to learn to recognise if a relationship has become toxic and bad for us. If we can't change their behaviours towards us, we must be brave enough to walk away and look for new more fulfilling relationships where both people can flourish.

Personality type

There are quite a few personality tests around. A simple but effective one we tend to use at Karis is from a book called *Personality Plus* by Florence Littauer.[6] When the girls have been with us a while and have stopped being so focused only on themselves and their needs, we introduce this personality test. It generates a great deal of interest and it has some helpful insights. My friend Marion and I, who have worked closely together for over twenty years, were surprised at how accurate the outcomes were, not just about ourselves, but about how we relate to one another. This has proved invaluable in understanding our differences, but also in getting the girls to understand why they relate to some people much better than oth-

---

6   F Littauer, *Personality Plus: How to understand others by understanding yourself* (Revell, 1992)

ers. It has helped understanding of one another in the house and improved team working in the workplace.

I tend to process quickly and want to get things done as soon as I have an idea. Marion wants to think about things and look at it from all angles. Sometimes her cautious nature has saved me from making a disastrous mistake; at other times it frustrates me, and we can have what we call 'heated moments of relationship'. In fact, our different personalities have complimented one another over many years, both at work, in church and in our personal lives. This has allowed both of us to experience and achieve much more than we would have done alone.

Why we were so different in our approaches was partly explained when we did the personality test outlined by Florence Littauer. We discovered that I was apparently a cross between a Popular Sanguine and a Powerful Choleric, both of whom are noisy optimists. The Sanguine wants to be in the middle of everything, and loves being around people and telling elaborate stories. The Choleric wants to get things done quickly and is seen as a born leader.

Marion identified predominantly as a Peaceful Phlegmatic combined with Melancholic, so she was detail orientated. She is a quiet introvert, a watcher and thinker who doesn't always feel the need to plan ahead. She adjusts to change more easily and likes to take time over decisions, aware of how others might be feeling when moving quickly in decision making. No wonder we struggle with each other's way of working sometimes, although most of the time our different approaches work well for us and those around us.

This revelation of my personality made a lot of sense and allowed me the freedom to continue to just be myself instead of striving to be like others. I used to envy people who could sit quietly in a group and not speak. I wondered what they were thinking and sometimes even found it a bit unnerving, especially as, try as I might, I cannot keep quiet. It bothered me for a long time, until I did the personality test. This also helped to remind me that God created me as I am. He made me uniquely for the purpose He had already prepared in advance for my life. If I was like Marion, I couldn't do the job He has put me in right now, and if she was like me she couldn't do hers.

SUSIE

Doing the personality test was also helpful when it came to understanding Susie. Since she had been with us she had come out of her shell quite a lot, but she was still slow to divulge any information about herself to anyone, even the girls that she lived with. She also struggled with a low mood, even though she had been working well through her issues to the extent that she was now undertaking professional training.

Compared with when she arrived, she was relatively happy. She felt like she belonged and could function day to day, even forming good relationships with others, but she didn't seem to have any real high points in her life. After we did her personality test, we realised that she scored incredibly high on just the Melancholic scale, whereas most people have predominantly two or more traits. This personality describes people who are introverted, known to avoid being singled out in a crowd, and self-reliant; they are thoughtful, reserved and often anxious. They are deep thinkers and feelers. This described Susie perfectly.

Recognising that the traits we had been concerned about were fundamentally her personality, albeit slightly exacerbated by her issues in the past, it was easier to help her move forward. We were able to encourage her to accept that her mood, while possibly appearing low at times, was part of her reflective personality. The Perfect Melancholic apparently naturally tends to have a negative attitude that finds a problem in every situation, again something that Susie certainly struggles with. As a lighter side to this we discovered that someone had attributed personality types to all the *Winnie-the-Pooh* characters and Susie's character was definitely Eeyore, the donkey who apparently has depression. Whenever she began to slip too far into negativity, we pulled her out by referencing her affinity to him and she would protest loudly. It's pretty hard to stay completely negative and quiet when you're being aligned to a grey donkey. Whatever works!

It would take up too much time here to go into personality types in detail and there are plenty of other books specialising in this very subject, so I'm not going to describe them all. I will say, though, that when we understand our girls' personalities it does help how we approach some things with them. We also discovered that allocating some of the day-to-day roles for staff in the house was made easier by recognising their strengths in areas dependent on their personalities.

Understanding your own personality type, and the traits that might bring, can help you understand why you respond a certain way in some situations. It can also help you recognise why others behave the way they do. It can take the pressure off when you are trying to behave a certain way if that is not something comfortable for your personality type, such as having to lead when you're not a natural leader. Recognising that different personalities react in different ways and that neither way is right or wrong allows us to function without fear of judgement. Understanding our own and others' personalities helps us to respond more appropriately to others. It doesn't mean we can't do things outside our normal personality traits; it just may not be as comfortable for us.

Our personality also affects how we process information. A lively outgoing personality will often also be quick to both process and respond in any given situation, although, as ever, this is not definitive. Some quieter personalities might process just as quickly but choose not to respond in the moment, or indeed at all.

Some people of any personality type can be said to 'jump to conclusions' quickly. These can be positive and happy conclusions or, as is often the case in our girls at Karis, negative conclusions, often about themselves or others.

Sometimes the way or the speed at which we process situations may be due to highly tuned survival instincts from earlier life situations, a learned behaviour for protection. Recognising when someone is becoming angry or knowing what will trigger this can have been learned in response to a parent who perhaps became violent following alcohol. Maybe the parent had a 'short fuse' because of stress or tiredness, so that even little things not working might have triggered outrage. Children come to recognise the signs in order to keep themselves safe and may then carry this into adulthood. Sometimes they know why, but often they do not recognise or remember the need that precipitated this behaviour; they just know that they gather and process this information automatically.

It doesn't have to have occurred in childhood – a violent partner will alter how someone processes information, as I mentioned when talking about my first husband. It may manifest as needing to sit near a door to know there is an escape route or on the end of a row in a large gathering for a fear of being trapped. Processing emotions in these situations can leave us with a distorted understanding. Not knowing how to respond emotionally then can stay with us and confuse how we recognise emotions in us and others in the future.

Fear is a powerful emotion and it can interfere with the thinking even of those who are ordinarily logical people. Fear of punishment or fear of losing someone can interfere with the way the mind processes information. One person in a relationship can be speaking and it appears that the other person is listening. In reality, what they are hearing may not be what is actually being said.

We have one-to-one time with our girls at Karis in which we explore their past with them. We take time to build good relationships so that we can guide them through their past until we find the trigger for whatever has got them to where they are today, unable to cope with living independently. Then we gently help them to unravel the lies they've believed from that time forward and often added to over time. This involves challenging some core beliefs for them; often these are negative views of who they are and why.

One of the big problems here is that if you have believed something for a long time it has been added to over time and become distorted further. It's like getting a simple sum wrong – if you make two plus two equal five, then multiply and add and continue to do that, no matter how good your maths afterwards, the end answer will always be wrong because of that early mistake. Unfortunately, this is the case for many of our girls – an early wrong belief about who they are is compounded as they, and others, go on adding to it.

When you believe you're rubbish and that you come from nowhere and you're going nowhere, the way you process information is different. Unless we are careful with the way we say things, the girls can process what they hear in a negative way. This is usually in a way that involves putting themselves down or believing that we are putting them down. This is, for many of them, their default thinking pattern; their thought processing always has them in the wrong, or incorrectly perceived to be in the wrong. Sometimes, no matter how hard you try, they jump to the conclusion that they are wrong or not wanted or maybe worthless. How they process impacts their view of everything.

LISA

You will remember Lisa, who was abandoned by her birth mother and abused by her adoptive father. She completely believed that her only role in life was to serve others. No matter how hard we tried to say things in a way that did not place blame on her, she always assumed that everything that went wrong was her fault. This was based on the fact that most of the key adults in her childhood had let her down in some way, so she believed that obviously she must have done something terribly wrong.

When she later tried to attach herself to another family, she was abused again. This just confirmed her lack of worth, her role of having been created purely to serve others proven in her eyes.

Trying to address her unhealthy coping strategies without her closing down completely and assuming blame for behaviours which were not her fault was difficult. It is a fine balancing act to challenge someone while not damaging their self-esteem further.

This is the same for many people and, if it goes unchallenged, people will go on processing day-to-day conversations through distorted thinking. They don't have a sense of individual identity and this can become a real challenge. If we don't know who we are or what we stand for, people can take advantage of us; they can tell us what to believe and we have no way of countering it. Today's culture increases the risk of this. Everywhere we look, on Facebook, television, YouTube, all social media in fact, everyone else looks perfect, as if their lives are idyllic. This makes our imperfect lives look all the more disappointing. It is also so much harder these days to identify the truth as there is so much 'fake news' and so many sophisticated scams out there, which leaves everyone open to manipulation.

Unforgiveness

Unforgiveness can be one of the single most destructive emotions. When people have been hurt, they often feel that they cannot forgive the person who hurt them because they believe it would be letting them off the hook. Nothing could be further from the truth. In reality, the other person often has no idea, or worse still doesn't care, that you still don't forgive them. Unforgiveness is so toxic that Joyce Meyer describes it as you taking poison and hoping the other person dies.[7] It seeps into everything you think and do and colours every decision you make, whether you know it or not. Even when we have forgotten about something that happened a long time ago, we can still find ourselves upset out of all proportion. We can be unnecessarily fearful or angry unexpectedly when something triggers a memory of what happened. While we hang on to negative feelings towards the person who hurt us, we continue to allow that hurt to go on. We make vows to ourselves to never let them off the hook, when in reality it is we who are still dangling on their hook.

In some cases, they may not even remember who we are. They did their damage and left without a backward glance and are certainly not thinking about us now. While we are still thrown whenever we think about what they did, and maybe suffer sleepless nights over it, they are fine. If they feel any guilt, they are certainly not telling you about it. Sometimes, sadly all too often, the perpetrator is someone within the family or friendship circle and hasn't actually physically gone. This can be harder still as they may continue as normal, while you feel the weight of your

---

7   J Meyer, *Beauty for Ashes: Receiving emotional healing* (FaithWords, 2003)

unforgiveness. They even may have forgotten about it, or are hoping you have; either way, the fact that you hold so much unforgiveness towards them is still only hurting you, not them.

I'm not saying you should rush to them and tell them you've forgiven them and want to start again and maybe place yourself in a risky situation, not at all. I'm not talking about reconciliation, here. I'm talking about the damage and pain of holding on to unforgiveness in your heart, of reliving something in your mind over and over. There obviously may be some situations where forgiveness could lead to reconciliation, but that depends on many other factors, which we will look at further on.

There may have been times when you wondered where God was in a bad situation. You may wonder why He didn't appear at the time to help you out of a desperate place. You may have been disappointed or angry at Him for not answering your prayers. All of these can leave you with unforgiveness towards God. This not only causes the normal harm that unforgiveness creates but has the added disadvantage of separating you from Him. The devil loves it when we blame God – it allows him free rein to help us destroy our lives.

Regret

There are some lovely quotes on social media (yes, it does have *some* good points) about never being too old to try something new – it's never too late to change – the best time to start is now. They obviously have a strong element of truth in them, but for some people that is not how they see it. Some feel that they have missed the boat, their lifelong dreams have never transpired, and they feel it is too late to do anything about it now. This is really sad and a great loss to the world of their skills and talents and whatever they might have achieved. Some of this is down to disillusionment over unfulfilled dreams, either because of other commitments getting in the way or maybe other people making demands and making them feel their dreams were unachievable or unimportant. The realisation that many opportunities have passed you by can lead to a depressive mood, which can take away all motivation. Regret at what you haven't achieved can override all the good things you may have done and your sadness at recognising this loss can leave you powerless to recover and try anything new at this stage; you feel it's all too late. How sad to never quite achieve your dreams. How much worse to stop trying for that before you really should.

Sometimes people's confidence takes a knock when they retire, or their children leave home. If their identity is wrapped up in what they do – their work, parenting or homemaking – they might find it hard to start something new to either occupy their time or to fulfil something they've always wanted to do. They may feel undermined and of little value. The more these thoughts take hold, the harder it is to reverse them and step out in a new area. It's often covered with jokes of 'I've done my bit', but in truth they would love to do more and are afraid to step out. While the media is beginning to recognise that this should be encouraged, it isn't making it that easy yet.

Summary

In this chapter we have identified a range of additional things that can contribute to who we are today. We have discovered that our perception will change how we behave and that our personality will have a bearing on that and how we process information. We've also learned that mistakes made early on in our lives about who we are can be compounded by ongoing mistaken beliefs and hold us back.

'Do not be anxious about anything, but in every situation, by prayer and petition, with thanksgiving, present your requests to God. And the peace of God, which transcends all understanding, will guard your hearts and your minds in Christ Jesus.'
— Philippians 4:6–7

STEP UP actions

Spend time with God

Now is a good moment to spend some time with God. To do this, find a quiet space with no distractions and ask Him to bring to mind what He wants you to consider.

Think about what you've just read

Discover which aspects of this chapter apply to you.

Explore the relevance to you

Write down anything that you believe is relevant. List both the negative things and the positive things that have become part of who you are today.

Pray about it

Let's pray for God to prepare your heart to work to overcome any negative effects of these events. You can use the prayer below to get started or pray in your usual way to God, whichever feels most comfortable to you.

Father God, we know that You love us the way we are, but that You love us too much to leave us that way. Be with me as I discover which aspects found in this chapter are having a negative impact on my life right now and help me to make changes. Soften my heart, Lord, and allow me to be honest with myself. Thank you, Lord. Amen.

Uncover scriptures that speak to you

Write scriptures on Post-it notes or coloured card and put them all around the house or in your pocket to support your journey.

Personal journal

Write about the outcomes in your personal journal to remind you just how far you've come on the days when you need encouragement.

PART THREE
RECOVER THE REAL YOU

We are now at the start of Part Three. You have worked through so much in the first two parts about how you became a little bit broken. Here you will recover the real you as you continue on your healing journey.

6
How Do I Become Me?

Well done you! You have come through the most difficult part. I hope that during the previous parts of the book you have had some 'aha' moments, either while reading the text or in carrying out the STEP UP actions at the end of each chapter. While the journey to this moment may have been uphill, you have now made so much progress towards your healing. You have laid a new foundation for full understanding. Well done.

Let's continue our journey. Let's move to the part you've really been waiting for: how to make sense of all we've talked about up to now, and how to fully recover the real you. How do I make all this meaning-ful in a way that allows me to live free of the things that have held me back and contained me? How do I become the me I always wanted to be? How do I stop being a little bit broken? I hope what we are going on to look at will help trigger many more 'lightbulb' moments for you as everything falls into place.

Understanding

The first step forward in all of this is getting to know yourself better, and understanding why you behave the way you do in any given situation. That is why I've devoted so many chapters to exploring many of the possible scenarios that can have impacted where you are today. Even if you are functioning relatively okay, and many people do despite some horrendous events in their lives, you can always improve. Whatever we are doing, wherever we are at, there's no doubt there is always room for improvement, even in so-called 'high functioning' individuals, so don't be too hard on yourself if you're not perfect yet. None of us is.

If you were able to recognise any of the issues dogging your life from the previous chapters, you are already part way there. If not, don't despair, as all may become clear in the coming chapters. We all function differently and for some people the things we explored there will have been known to them, even though they don't know how to do anything about it. For others there may have been a realisation of the reason they behaved in certain ways. For still others, nothing may have resonated or appeared to relate to them at all. This may be for several reasons. They may have been firmly directed by parents, carers or abusers to never speak of certain things – these are secrets not to be shared for fear of retribution. Maybe they have subconsciously chosen to block these things from the conscious memory to cope with day-to-day living, or they don't really believe that what happened to them in the past has any bearing on how they behave today.

So whether we know about the things from our past that are impacting us or not, we do need to try to explore areas from back then that are uncomfortable in order to reach an understanding of their impact on us today. If you are one of the people who doesn't feel that anything in earlier chapters rang any bells for you, keep reading, because maybe something will be triggered or begin to make sense for you anyway. It's surprising how things can fall into place when we least expect it. You may also benefit from taking a little more time with God. It would be good to come aside, away from any distractions, and spend some private time in prayer, asking God to reveal to you anything you haven't yet seen. Our protective mechanisms can sometimes be incredibly effective, and we need to give God every opportunity to help us discover any-thing that may be relevant.

However, if you are already completely happy with who you are and genuinely content with your life, don't go looking for things that may just not be there.

This may be either because you have had a great life so far, or you have already come to terms with issues from your past. Be grateful that you haven't had to deal with the situations I've described here; fortunately, there are many others like you.

If you have faced things but already overcome them, give yourself a pat on the back for that; it's not an easy thing to do. You may even have been specifically thinking of someone else when you bought this book; if not, maybe you need to look around and see if there's someone you know who could do with your help right now. Even if you simply give them a copy of the book, perhaps it could be a conversation starter if you suspect they are struggling with issues from their past.

Overcoming

Overcoming something as a whole can be difficult, but breaking it down and looking at it from all perspectives can help us on the journey. One of the key things we do with our girls at Karis is to pull out the issues that cause them the most problems day to day and explore them from every angle. Obviously, for many of us there are several key things that have occurred in our lives, but to begin with it's good to just focus on one. Move on to the others after each one is dealt with, and in many cases, resolved. Sometimes the memory is an incredibly painful one and has never been discussed with anyone else. Often this is because the expectation is that the person it's shared with will see them in a different, negative light. This secrecy, brought about by fear, gives much more power to the memory, no matter how big or small. It's important to remember that, even if the issue seems unimportant to others, if it has a life-controlling effect on the person involved then it still needs dealing with and should be taken seriously.

One of the early things we were taught when I was a nursing student was that pain is what the patient perceives it to be, regardless of whether we think there should be pain. This holds true, not only for physical pain, but for mental anguish too. If we are the one with a painful past experience that is affecting our life, we must give ourselves the respect we would give others. We should accept that the issue is important, even if it seems silly on the surface. I would venture to suggest that many people don't deal with their issues for this very reason and think they should just 'get over it'. The truth is that if it's still interfering with how you live your life then you haven't. You won't until you give yourself a break and do something to help yourself get over it, whatever 'it' is.

HOLLY

Holly felt that some of her past issues had been partly her fault and so she should just get over them, but as we began to work through them, taking them apart and looking at them from many angles, she came to recognise that some of her decisions at that time were in response to the circumstances she found herself in. We explored various other ways she could have reacted at the time and whether they would have left her in a better condition to cope now. We also looked at the possible reasons she would worry so much about her mum and why her dad may have responded to her the way he did. This allowed her to recognise that his responses were probably proportionate to the risk he as an adult saw for her mum. Maybe he just didn't recognise or accept the depth of worry Holly was feeling for her mum at the time. As we considered different viewpoints, she found that the discussions and these new possible perspectives took the power out of the issues that had weighed heavily on her before.

Having unpicked her and other people's thought processes around them, she began to really move forward in every area. The new realisation that she could look at an issue from many viewpoints instead of just her own seemed to free her from fixating on one perspective and allowing her fears to spiral out of control. She began to use this tool in many situations to help her make more balanced decisions and overcome her tendency to make spontaneous, sometimes unwise, choices.

Looking at an incident from our more distant past, maybe in childhood, and examining it from different angles allows us to view it through both our childhood eyes and our adult eyes. As a child there are many things we don't know about, for example our parents' relationships with one another or what the finances were like in our childhood home. In many instances we don't know if our parents were ill, overly controlled by their parents or influenced by friends. There may have been enormous pressures that we, as a child, didn't understand. When a parent ignored or shouted at us or drank too much and lashed out we were left afraid and alone. We were unable to process any extra information going on in the background to help ourselves understand. As a child all we felt was pain, confusion and helplessness, which we inevitably carry with us into adulthood. Unless we make a deliberate effort to process this later it can lay dormant, like a virus, and rear up to infect us if we find ourselves in another situation where we feel helpless or afraid. If you heard parents shouting at one another downstairs in childhood and this preceded violence towards you, the child, in adulthood people shouting might put you more on edge than most people. You may anticipate physical violence towards you following shouting; even if your mind has hidden the actual childhood memory, the fear may remain. Our past experiences can create an expectation – it's like a form of programming.

This is a simplified example on purpose, to get the point across. However, I hope you can see how, if you break down some of the issues from your past and see them in the light of reasoned explanation, you can perhaps make more sense of them. This might make them easier to overcome. Don't get me wrong, I'm absolutely not condoning the behaviour of any parent who treats their children in this way. In some instances, however, there are simple explanations which may make the memory of them easier to overcome. We can look at it in a similar way to waking in the night and being fearful of something lurking in the dark. Children often see monsters in the shapes of things on the floor in the dark. When you wake suddenly, it can be frightening if you can't make out what something really is. When we turn the light on, though, we can see that the monster was in reality just a teddy bear, a ball and a book all leaning at funny angles on each other. The truth, while maybe still not pleasant, is not always as scary as we thought. Sometimes this is what we can discover if we look at an issue from our past with fresh eyes. While it caused us harm back then when we were in the dark, it has no power over us now that we are in the light. Breaking issues down this way and looking at them in a fresh light is a really good step to overcoming things that are holding us back.

SALLY

Returning to Sally, you may remember that she had a difficult time at home with her mum's boyfriend, so much so that she had to move out. She also found herself in an unpleasant ongoing situation with a group of so-called friends. The sense of rejection and shame she felt at that time, while she attempted to bury it, led to various other events before she finally came to us.

One of the things that really helped Sally was to explore each of these issues and look at them from all angles. She came to understand that maybe her mum had not fully realised the impact the boyfriend's behaviour had on Sally. Even if she had recognised the issues to some degree, maybe her mum was too fearful to risk going back to being on her own with three children to stand up to him. Possibly his manipulation was so good that her mum thought Sally was saying things out of jealousy. She considered the thought that maybe the boyfriend extended his abusive behaviour towards her mum and she was afraid of him too, especially as the relationship broke up eventually.

It was too late to change anything now but considering these possibilities helped Sally to feel a little less hurt by the whole thing. As a side note, Sally and her mum are fully reconciled now and have a good relationship.

There are obviously situations that impact us negatively in adulthood, too, as we identified earlier. Some of these may be huge and life changing, but some can just be little niggles that rub and make us feel unhappy, like feeling excluded or overlooked. The principles explored above around the child not knowing the full story can still have a basis here. It may be that even as an adult we don't know the full background in a given situation. These can also be worked through more easily if we break them down and look at them from all the different points of view of those involved. Sometimes this can give us a fresh eye on what happened, or a greater understanding of why it happened. Even if it still doesn't feel as though we were treated right, this new insight can help us to come to terms with it more easily.

If this is too hard to do alone, we can talk with a trusted friend as an outsider to the event, which, if the friend is chosen wisely, can help bring a new perspective. On talking something through with a close friend on one occasion, I was given a useful piece of advice, and I share it with all the girls. It was a relatively small issue, really, but it was causing me quite a bit of emotional pain. Someone with whom I'd previously had a pretty close relationship suddenly started ignoring me completely with no explanation. I racked my brains to try to remember what I might have done to upset her but couldn't come up with anything.

I was sharing my distress over it with a friend and she pointed out that it wasn't always about me. Maybe that person was having struggles of her own and wasn't ignoring me but was just wrapped up in her own issues. I began to consider all the possible things that could have been going on for her, and there could have been many reasons. It was a lesson I've never forgotten. Now I always try to give people the benefit of the doubt; maybe they just had a fight with their partner, or they're not well, or they're worried about an elderly parent – the possibilities are endless. It's not always about you.

Forgiveness

All that said, there are things that happen to us that no amount of breaking down is going to help us overcome, even if it might make some sense of them. In many of these circumstances our only real option is forgiveness. I said earlier that unforgiveness is like you taking poison and hoping the other person dies. Unforgiveness seeps into our whole lives, leaving us continually licking wounds, bringing up old hurts, holding grudges and even plotting revenge. All of these things and more continue to impact us negatively. Once we have come to an understanding of what happened, it's important that we find a way to overcome it and rebuild our sense of safety.

At this point many people are thinking that the awful things done to them cannot possibly just be forgiven. They feel that if they forgive them, their abuser will be getting away with what they did. Unfortunately, in many of these situations they already have. Many of these abusers are people from your past who deliberately or accidently harmed you. In most instances it is too late to actually do anything about that, and while you believe that holding onto the anger you feel towards them is somehow evening the score, it isn't. It is only continuing to damage you; for the most part they have no idea, or worse, don't care what you think. In many instances, the only place the incident still has any life is in your memory. It's still disturbing you, still playing out in your mind. Isn't it time to close that door and move forwards, so you can feel safe again and be free of the offence?

Simply forgiving someone is really difficult for most of us. Everyone struggles with it because of all we've discussed above, and maybe other more personal reasons. Nevertheless, it is still a big step towards personal freedom and peace. Forgiving someone is something you do entirely for you. It takes away the power of the event or of that person over you. Effectively, you are taking back control, which is one of the things lost in many careless or abusive actions. Whether someone is deliberately or unwittingly impacting your life negatively, you will feel out of control. As we discussed earlier, we react in all manner of potentially self-harming ways to regain that control.

Sometimes we know why, sometimes we don't, and we are not even always aware that we are doing it. If you can understand that forgiving someone gives you back control over that area of your life then it begins to make sense that this is what you need to do. Forgiveness brings personal transformation because the weight of unforgiveness is so immense. While we are carrying around bitterness in our hearts for what others have done to us, we are weighed down. We are not able to enjoy life fully because in some sense we are still connected to that person and the pain that was inflicted in our past, even if it is the fairly recent past.

You are not saying that what happened wasn't important, that it wasn't bad or sad; you are saying, 'I've had enough of this controlling me, and I'm taking back control.' You are freeing yourself of something that no longer has a place in your life. You want to be free of it so you must forgive and let it go. This may not be a one-off event, either. You will probably find yourself having to do this again and again. It is a choice, but because it is such a hard choice to make, you may slip back from time to time, especially at the beginning, but you must persevere, because the final outcome is worth it. The longer you live in this forgiveness, the easier it becomes, and the less you have to make a conscious choice about it, as eventually it becomes second nature, a part of you. Then, when you think about what happened (because you will, we're not talking about brainwashing or amnesia here) you will feel pride in your ability to overcome it instead of the pain that memory would have brought you before.

We need to remember here, also, that we don't have to do this alone; God will be with us and take the weight of this for us if we ask Him. He knows we need to do this and is just waiting to help us out. We need to forgive and leave the offence at the foot of the Cross, not keep taking it back as we all have a tendency to do. Once we've given it to Him to carry, we must walk away, even if we have to do that over and over to begin with.

One way to do this, if you like to get things out of your head, is to write a letter to the person you need to forgive. Tell them how they made you feel when they did those things to you. Tell them how you feel now and that you are going to set yourself free by forgiving them. Read the letter out loud, somewhere safe where you won't be heard. Then forgive them and pray for them and for yourself; ask God to help you continue to forgive. You may want someone you trust with you to do this. You need to destroy the letter by burning it or tearing it into tiny pieces. I wouldn't suggest keeping it or you may be tempted to go back to it and distress yourself all over again.

We talked earlier, too, about actually holding unforgiveness towards God for the bad things that have happened in our lives. We ask why He didn't stop them – where was He? The truth is that He was always there and probably saved us from much worse in each situation. We need to put down our unforgiveness towards Him and turn back to Him. He loves us unconditionally and would never harm us. He has given us and the rest of mankind free will, though, so sometimes we may be the victim of someone else's free will, or a poor choice on our part. While God cannot stop that because He would be taking away our free will, He can make good out of the situation, which I have seen Him do repeatedly. He also promises to always be with us, so no matter what we are going through we know we are never alone. He will strengthen and uphold us in every situation.

Something else we need to consider here is not just forgiving others but forgiving ourselves.

HOLLY

Let's return to Holly, who struggled with overwhelming anxiety when apart from her mother, so much so that she could no longer leave the house or manage at night because of her fears. As she worked through her feelings towards the girls at school who had bullied her, and forgave them for this, she moved on to a number of people she felt had harmed her in various ways, which had culminated in the anxiety and panic she felt. She looked at these from various angles and came to understand how each had impacted her.

She was ready to forgive them one after another, which she did. Her biggest problem was now forgiving herself for her part in all of this. She realised that she had made some bad choices along the way that had contributed to how some people had responded to her. Interestingly, although she was ready to forgive everyone else for their part in the build-up to her inability to cope, she found forgiving herself much more difficult. She came to understand that, although she may have made many mistakes in her journey, some were based on lies she'd believed about herself or others. Some were out of fear, believing she would be alone or abandoned if she didn't comply, and some were simply that she gave into temptation to do the wrong thing.

Recognising that she was not the only person to do these things and that, while they were not right, she would forgive other people for them, she realised eventually that she could let herself off the hook and forgive herself, while learning and making sure she tried not to make the same mistakes again. Soon after this, even more things started to come together for Holly, until she was finally ready to leave us. By the time she left she was confident on public transport, which she had not been able to use before as she was crippled with fear. She was also able to load her own car and drive the considerable distance home alone – something else she would never have managed previously.

Just like Holly, there are some situations where people have not done what they know to be right and have given in to temptation. Their desire to do or have something overrides their good judgement, resulting in poor choices. Unfortunately, bad choices usually carry consequences that can be long lasting. That said, we cannot go back and change what we did, so how do we cope? How can we move forward? Just as we would forgive others, we must learn to forgive ourselves. That doesn't mean we just forget what we did, far from it – we need to remember that slip-up, so it doesn't happen again. We shouldn't dwell on it, but if we find ourselves in similar situations in the future we can learn from those past mistakes.

In many abuse or trauma scenarios where the victim has no control, however, they can still have a faulty element of self-blame. 'If only I had said this or done that, things might have played out differently. It was my fault because I kept quiet about it. I caused it because I led them on, pushed too hard, didn't stop them...' No! Absolutely not! Whatever part you think you played, you did not deserve an outcome that would go on to cause you pain for many years to come. You are not to blame for what someone else did to you. I don't even need to know what happened to you to know for sure that it was not your fault. I have heard many stories like yours and it was never the victim's fault. Finally forgive yourself for the responsibility you thought you had for whatever happened. You were in the wrong place at the wrong time and, in many cases, it could have happened to almost anyone. Whatever you are holding against yourself right now, it is time to let it go. Believe it, forgive yourself, especially if, as is common, you thought you should have had the power to stop them. You need to forgive yourself over and over until you believe it. Forgiveness (of yourself or others) is one of the greatest gifts you can give yourself; decide to do that right now and keep on doing it until you no longer even think about it anymore. Time to walk free from unforgiveness.

Reconciliation

Some people assume that forgiveness means they must make up with the person who hurt them. This is not true, although a genuine heartfelt apology from them for what they did wrong can go a long way to making forgiveness easier. The truth is that reconciliation is not the same as forgiveness; they can be connected, but they are not the same, otherwise how could you forgive someone after they have died? It would mean that you would have to carry the unforgiveness for the rest of your life if this were the case. There are people who still won't recognise that what they did was wrong. If forgiveness depended on the perpetrator apologising and making things right, forgiveness would be out of reach of the victim. This would be unfortunate as many studies have identified that unforgiveness has a negative impact on people's health.[8] We must remember that forgiveness is for you; whether or not to seek reconciliation is also a decision for you to take.

Therefore, forgiveness is not dependent on reconciliation taking place. That being said, for some people reconciliation may be the desired outcome or natural progression from forgiveness, and there are several ways that this can occur. Obviously, there is a hope that total restoration of the relationship can take place in a way in which both people change and grow from the experience. In this instance deep mutual healing occurs, maybe transforming the relationship into more than it was before. This is the ideal and it takes a lot of work on the part of both parties involved, but the shared benefits are amazing.

---

8   L Toussaint, E Worthington & D Williams, *Forgiveness and Health: Scientific evidence and theories relating forgiveness to better health* (Springer, 2015)

There may be a way that the relationship can be reconciled but it may require one person in the relationship to make allowances. One may need to change their expectations of the other party because the other is unwilling or unable to make significant changes in their behaviour. Rather than lose the relationship altogether, one person may be prepared to make these changes. The final way that reconciliation can take place is if the two parties both just agree to disagree. This can occur if both people have a different recollection of what happened in the past. Rather than battling over who is right and trying to convince one another, the two people can just agree to differ. The reconciliation is forged on new memories being built together that have no connection to the initial disagreement.

There may, sadly, be situations in which reconciliation is too difficult even if forgiveness has been reached in the victim and reconciliation is desired. The perpetrator may still be a threat to the victim, which would render reconciliation too dangerous.

LISA

Lisa had come to understand that holding onto her anger over what her adoptive parents had done to her was causing her more harm. It was contributing to an inability to sleep and nightmares as she just couldn't understand why they had both behaved the way they had. She had a deep desire to get even, but it was eating away at her. There was no way we could help her to understand why they treated her that way because we simply didn't know; no one could. We could offer potential reasons, but they were suppositions and generalisations. The only thing we could realistically do in this situation was to explain the power of forgiveness and show her how she could learn to forgive them. While she wasn't exactly thrilled at this idea, over time and with prayer she finally felt ready to take the big step of forgiving them both. She had written a letter to each of them addressing their part in hurting her the way they did and telling them how it made her feel. These letters were never meant to be sent; they were just a way of expressing feelings. As she read them aloud, she sobbed, but as she told them why she had found it so hard to forgive them we saw the relief begin to flood over her face. Once she had finished, she prayed for God to take the pain of those memories and to keep her strong in her forgiveness of them. We took the letters outside and she burnt them.

Over the next few days, with that burden lifted, the change in her was immense. Then, after a few months, the adoptive mother tried to contact her for the first time since she had left their home. Lisa was so confused and overwhelmed with trying to decide whether to allow the contact after what had happened in the past. Her desire to have a mother figure in her life was so strong that she considered it. Having forgiven them, she thought she might be able to meet with them safely, on her terms. As the time to make contact grew nearer, she became distressed and her nightmares returned. Her anxiety and fear of what might happen grew until she could no longer cope. After incredibly careful, prayerful consideration we agreed with Lisa that reconciliation was not possible in this instance. The risk of her being harmed in some way again was just too great, although Lisa was able to continue in her forgiveness of them once this situation was settled.

Forgiveness is essential for your health, but reconciliation is not the same thing and does not automatically follow. Apart from reconciliation possibly being dangerous, it may not be possible for other reasons. We may not know where the other person is, or they may have died. Under these circumstances reconciliation is, of course, impossible.

Summary

In this chapter we have begun to identify what we need to do to begin to break free from the events and issues of our past that are still impacting us. This part of our healing journey has given us understanding so that we can overcome these things. We have discovered that we need to forgive those whom we perceive harmed us in the past and, where safe and possible, may seek reconciliation.

> 'Trust in the Lord with all of your heart and lean not on your own understanding; in all your ways submit to Him, and He will make your paths straight.'
> — Proverbs 3:5–6

STEP UP actions

Spend time with God

Now is a good moment to spend some time with God. To do this, find a quiet space with no distractions and ask Him to bring to mind what He wants you to consider.

Think about what you've just read

To recover you need to choose which aspects of this chapter apply to you. You may have several issues to overcome; work through them one at a time. You may also have several people to forgive; again, work through them one at a time.

Take your time – this is not a race and may be hard for you to do. If you feel overwhelmed, take a break and spend some time with God. You may feel that it would be helpful to have someone you trust with you as you work through this part. You may need several attempts depending on your situation.

Explore the relevance to you

If you need to understand something from your past, write down all you remember from that time. Ask any questions you had back then and try to answer them for yourself, looking from a different perspective. (From someone else involved at the time, maybe.)

If you have people you need to forgive, including yourself, write them a letter saying everything you needed to say then and now. Do not send it to them, but spend time later reading through this in prayer with God.

Write down anything that you believe is relevant. List both the negative things and the positive things that have become part of who you are today.

Pray about it

When you feel ready, pray and forgive them out loud. Some people find it helpful to burn this letter or tear it into small pieces and scatter it into a river as they pray and forgive.

Let's pray for God to be with you and uphold you while you do this difficult but freeing process. You can use the prayer below to get started or pray in your usual way to God, whichever feels most comfortable to you.

Father God, I thank You that You are here with me and supporting me through this difficult task. Strengthen me as I work to overcome my past and to forgive those who hurt me. I pray right now to forgive _____ for _____ (enter relevant names and actions) and ask that You help me to do this today and every day from now on. Thank you, Lord. Amen.

Uncover scriptures that speak to you

Write scriptures on Post-it notes or coloured card and put them all around the house or in your pocket to support your journey.

Personal journal

Write about the outcomes in your personal journal to remind you just how far you've come on the days when you need encouragement.

7
Where Do I Go Now?

The STEP UP at the end of the last chapter may have taken you some time. I hope it was useful for you, even though it may have been hard. Ideally, you have reached a place of understanding and forgiveness that will allow you to participate fully in all that comes next. This chapter is about helping you to consolidate your freedom and healing.

Acceptance

Acceptance is an active decision on your part to tolerate something that you would actually rather change – coming to terms with what happened in your past, despite the fact that you would not have chosen what happened to you. It's a realisation that, although you have been changed by the situation, you have to allow yourself to leave it in the past so you can move on or it will go on damaging you. It is sometimes really hard to achieve because it's difficult to let go of things that have harmed us. Also, to reach it there has to first be an acknowledgement that the problem exists. How can you accept that there's a problem if you are unable or unwilling to see it? Some people struggle with acceptance because of this, but, if you have worked through your issues and used the STEP UP actions at the end of each chapter in the book so far, you should be beyond denial now.

Acceptance isn't a one-off action, either; sometimes you may need to revisit the decision again and again. Having overcome the issues from your past, though, you have now, hopefully, reached a place of acceptance that, although what happened was not good, it can't be changed. This acceptance will allow you to grow in freedom. Once you have truly come to terms with what happened, you are ready to consider your next steps.

LISA

Lisa really wanted to have the kind of mother she imagined for herself. She confessed to having idealised what this would look like from films and television. She wanted someone to tell her that they loved her and would always look out for her. She imagined having her mum come and tuck her in and kiss her goodnight. To have her mum waiting outside school so she could run to her and get a hug to make her feel safe, wanted and loved. The problem was that Lisa was already in her late twenties. Obviously, this was not going to happen.

She confessed that she absolutely hated seeing anyone else with a loving mother as this made her so intensely jealous that she could barely contain herself. As we unpacked this together, she got at first very angry with her birth mother for deserting her, then decided she needed to meet with her. She wanted to find out why she left her in the first place. Having received her file from Social Services, we went through what had actually happened. Lisa did not know all the facts about her past until then. When she found a sentence saying her mum had not wanted her and her siblings to go into care, she became defensive of her mum. It took her a while to work through the appalling conditions she had been found in before she realised that her mum was completely unable to look after her or her siblings.

Not to be dissuaded from her mission to reinstate a mother in her life, she began to idealise her adoptive mother again. She had ceased contact with the adoptive mother when she left her care at sixteen and again recently when the adoptive mother had tried to reconnect. Gently, she was reminded of the reasons she had made that choice. Over time, Lisa came to recognise for herself that her desire to be mothered during her childhood was no longer possible to fulfil. That time had passed, and while she could build a family of her own in the future, she could never be mothered in the way she wanted. This acceptance was a long process for her, but eventually she recognised it. She made an active decision to tolerate something she would rather have changed, allowing her to start a new chapter in her life. She made a choice to let go of something that could never be, in the hope of a better future.

Acceptance can change the direction of our lives dramatically when we make that choice. While it is a choice, it is impossible to pretend to accept something when in your heart you don't really believe it, because you will create a continual battle in your mind. Lisa had to try several times before she came to the genuine acceptance that neither of her mothers could fulfil the desire for the kind of mothering she had pictured. She was in real emotional turmoil during this battle because externally she had accepted it but internally she had not. One of the things that finally helped her to full acceptance of the situation was a fresh commitment to Jesus. Reminding herself of who she was in Christ let her know that she was not fighting this alone.

The first thing you need to consider with regards to *where* you are now is *who* you are now, especially if you prayed the prayer in the introduction. Remembering who you are in Christ will give you a new confidence. You need to know that you are not alone. When we have had struggles it can be hard to believe that our identity is wrapped up in Christ's. When we've believed negative things others have said about us and those things we may have said about ourselves, it seems hard to comprehend. It is, however, the truth. We have to begin to truly see ourselves through His eyes, not our own or the eyes of those in the world. The scripture list at the end of this chapter contains just some of the many truths contained in the Bible concerning our secure position in Christ, but you can always find more. Our role is to believe this, so we can live in the freedom this gives us to have a relationship with God in His great grace and mercy. Grace is not getting what we deserve when we mess up; mercy is getting what we don't deserve, which is given to us anyway. What a loving God.

We must know and accept what God thinks of us because that will give us the power we need to flourish in our new-found freedom. If we hold onto or slip back to our old understanding of who we are then we are effectively arguing with God. We are telling Him that He is wrong about us and we know better. We have to wonder, though: how can we know better than Him who created us in His own image? We must let go of who we thought we were and hold on to who God's Word says we are.

SALLY

As Sally was coming to the end of her time at Karis, she began to panic a little. I did a video interview with her to show at her finishing celebration at church. During this she expressed her concerns about who she would be now because she only knew herself as unwell. Despite the fact that God had moved mightily in her life and healed her both physically and psychologically, she still struggled to fully let go of who she had been. Some days she was afraid of whether old friends would accept her as she was now, even though she knew she had become a new creation in Him.

She had recommitted her life to Him and understood that He had freed her, and she really wanted to believe that, but some days it was hard. Sally had to learn to trust God with her whole being so that she could actually believe she was a new creation, every day. Sometimes that's not easy.

We need to apply God's Word about us in *every* area of our lives, then we can have a new-found confidence. If, like Sally, we struggle with that then we can return to God in prayer. If we ask Him to show us, He most certainly will. We can also go back into our Bibles where the Word of God will do us so much good. We need to learn it and hide it in our hearts so that it is there when we need reminding. Memorising scriptures that speak to you specifically is a really good way to give you the power you need to overcome in any situation.

Learning scripture is something the girls all do at Karis. At the breakfast table they share every morning the scripture that has spoken to them this week, which they have then chosen to learn. This might be one that God has brought to their attention through several mediums – someone giving them a scripture, or reading one in several places, or hearing the same one in a teaching. They also all have favourite scriptures that help them. One of the girls had Psalm 91, which she had written everywhere – it was a long one to remember. The length of it was helpful, though, because she would read it through slowly and would feel her anxiety lessen, then become calm again as she came to the end.

Belonging

We talked earlier about how important it is to feel like we belong. When we are a child of God we already belong in the family of God; we are heirs alongside Christ. This also gives us a chance to belong within a church setting. The church is not the building, it is the people, and we can be a part of that. When we become a church member we can belong to a much wider family. This is where we can develop new, healthy friendships. If our past issues have left us surrounded with toxic or negative people, here is a place we can develop new relationships. Toxic relationships will drag us back to our old negative coping strategies, so it is essential we look for new, more positive relationships once we have dealt with our past. The Bible says it is like a dog returning to its vomit when people go back to old negative behaviours. That would be counter-productive for you now you have come so far.

Obviously, church isn't the only place you can find good friendships, nor are all churches full of wholesome people, but it isn't a bad place to start. Usually you will find people who will encourage you and support your walk with the Lord. They will strengthen your faith, disciple you and help you learn to disciple others. This will give you opportunities for the personal connections we all crave. As I said earlier, we all want someone who 'gets' us. There is a universal need to be known, for some intimacy.

Before I gave my heart to Jesus, I didn't trust anybody. Most of my relationships were on a superficial level because I believed that would keep me safe. While it did do that, it was this very behaviour that led to my feeling so isolated much of the time. On the surface, it looked like I had many friends, but the only people who really knew me at all were my husband and daughter. A friend in the church helped me to see that we all need intimate relationships, in which people really get to know us. Someone once said that even the word intimacy says what it means if you think about it: in-to-me-see. Our most intimate relationship, though, will be with God because He knows all there is to know about us, yet still He loves us.

Freedom

What we do with our freedom once we've earned it is important. It has been a long journey to reach healing and freedom; we can't risk throwing it away or sliding backwards. We need time to consolidate our learning.

Freedom is a choice. Not a one-off choice, but a once-a-day choice. It may be even more than that to begin with or in specific areas that you struggle to stay free in. You may need to make good choices every hour – heck, I had a couple of things I had to make the choice on every minute, to begin with. I'm not a patient person and people taking an age to do what I consider to be simple things can drive me crackers. I'm learning to keep quiet, but it's taken me a long time and I still slip up occasionally. The choice can be made more difficult by how we feel, too. While God created our emotions – so they do have an important role to play in our lives – we can also let them run away with us. How we feel can often dictate how we behave, but that feeling may not be a true reflection of the situation. We must choose our faith over our feelings every time. When we feel angry, anxious or worried we need to check out the truth of God's Word against what we are feeling and, if it doesn't line up, we need to move on from it. For example, God's Word tells us many times not to fear or not to be afraid, but how many of us have to confess to periods of fear in our lives?

I want to look at something else we can use to help us make wise choices with regards to maintaining our hard-won freedom. One of the key tools we use with the girls at Karis is distraction. When we get tempted to make bad choices or we're starting to slide back into a negative mindset, distraction will help. The cards you have been writing scriptures on and placing in your home or pocket are a good distraction. They focus your mind away from the immediate problem. They will be even more effective if you learn them; in any given situation you can bring them to mind and say them to yourself silently. I have some that I use in the night if I cannot sleep because my mind has wandered somewhere it shouldn't go. This distraction will also help if we have a setback like an unexpected nightmare, flashback or bumping into someone negative we've already moved on from. We could be making all the right choices, but we have to accept that sometimes these things will still happen. We need to remember that we are more vulnerable to this if we are tired, hungry, lonely or unwell. Knowing this should help us to be mindful of the condition we let ourselves get into.

The girls at Karis have what we call distraction boxes, and it may be something you want to put together for yourself. They use them if any of the above things catch them unawares or if they are having trouble sleeping at night. They prepare them in advance of the possibility of this happening. They use wrapping paper to cover a shoe box or decorate it in some other way. Inside the box they put things that have a good meaning for them. Photos or articles with good memories attached, cards they've received or maybe music they like to listen to. Anything that makes them feel good when they see it. They add things like scent, nail varnish, hand cream, favourite sweets or something to stretch their minds like sudoku. These can all act as grounding as they feed into the senses, sight, taste, hearing, smell and touch. If they get upset or are struggling with anything, they will get their distraction box out and go through it. This usually calms them and makes them feel better about themselves so they don't do anything unwise or they can go peacefully to sleep. It's remarkably effective.

Many of the girls at Karis are creative, as am I. When I really struggled, poetry was my release, but I love doing all kinds of artwork, too, and I love to sing. We have found that creativity of some form seems to be a bit of a by-product of prior troubles, although of course it doesn't follow that you have to have had troubles before you can be creative. Creativity comes in many guises and we have had girls who are brilliant at furniture restoration, drawing, painting and writing. We've had a couple of amazing bakers. There have also been girls who love to sing or play an instrument. This creativity can also work like the distraction box, but it has an output as well. The girls are so talented that we now sell crafts online and take the craft stall to events. Apart from keeping them busy it also gives them a sense of contributing to Karis.

If you used to have a skill when you were younger but don't do it anymore, have another go at it. Some of the girls have knitted squares for blankets and learned to crochet. One girl learned a language and some of the others love puzzles. There really is no limit to what you could do – you just have to convince yourself to try. These activities become absorbing and eat up time. This is a really good thing if you are someone who would focus on something negative otherwise. Doing a creative activity is a choice you can make to help you maintain your freedom. It could also be something you join a group to do – this has the added bonus of widening your friendship group. People are surprisingly friendly when you enjoy doing the same things as them.

Another good use of your time and enabling you to meet other people is to volunteer. Most churches have plenty of opportunities to volunteer, but so do charity shops and schools, and many other places. Find something you will really enjoy doing, otherwise you will not be able to sustain your commitment, which will make you feel like you've failed. Think carefully about what will suit your personality and skills before you commit to anything and don't be pushed into something that isn't right for you. If you don't like talking to strangers then working in a charity shop isn't for you, but you might really enjoy helping out in the children's area in church. Take time to look around and find the right volunteering opportunity for you.

For the girls at Karis, the opportunity to volunteer in one of our charity shops or the café gives them a new skill and something to put on their curriculum vitae when they've finished with us. It also keeps them occupied doing something worthwhile, making them feel like they are contributing to Karis, which of course they are. One of our girls gets anxious when talking to people she doesn't know because she can't anticipate how they will respond. She bakes like an angel, though, so she does this when the café is shut, which is great for the café but bad for my waistline. The shops and café help to fund us as we have no statutory funding. Many of our girls over time have gained invaluable experience by taking the lead in running a shop as they prepare to go into future work roles. It gives them a real sense of purpose.

Some of you may feel volunteering is not something you would want to commit to, but if you've been out of work for a while it's a really good way of moving back into that arena. Most places that take volunteers are grateful for whatever amount of time you can offer, so don't worry that you can't deliver what they require. Make it clear when you first show an interest what your boundaries are and how many hours you can give, and they will respect that. You will find a new sense of purpose and you will get more confident as time passes. It will stop you dwelling on the things of the past that you have now overcome and may prepare you for work later, if you wish. It will also make you feel good doing something for someone else. If you are not in work, volunteering is a really good choice to help you maintain your freedom.

Growth

Another area you could consider, to keep yourself occupied and prevent you from dwelling on the past, is some form of sport. We have a small gym in the grounds of Karis and the girls use it a lot, especially if they need to work off anger issues or anxiety. One of our girls who came to us in a wheelchair ended up running the London Marathon to raise money for Karis. If some of your coping strategies involve food, using the gym could be a healthier way to fulfil your ideas of how your body should look – always assuming you don't replace one obsessive coping strategy with another. If you get involved in a sport that is a team game, it's another opportunity to meet people and build friendships. Time to practise taking off that mask and meeting people as you really are.

Something else you might want to look at now you have come this far is extra training. This could be for a new career or just in an area that has always interested you. One of the problems with battling the ghosts of our past or even battling with ourselves is that it's tiring. When we're not behaving how we want to, and we're doing things we don't want to do, it can leave us exhausted. It's like we're fighting constantly because we're fighting both sides of the battle. The apostle Paul talks of struggling with this very thing, not doing what he should and doing what he shouldn't, so we shouldn't be too hard on ourselves when we do this. However, now that you have dealt with your issues you will not be doing that as much, so you will be less emotionally tired. This could give you the opportunity to do some studying. Maybe your new-found confidence will allow you to train for a completely new role, perhaps one that you wanted to do as a youngster but didn't have the courage. I was thirty-five years old when I qualified as a nurse. This was something I would have loved to have done at eighteen but I didn't dare tell anyone then because I thought they would laugh at me. I have also just started studying for my master's degree in psychology. It's never too late to start something new, including a new career.

Transformation

At this point I expect that you are experiencing transformation, like our girls do before they leave Karis. Now you have recognised and dealt with things that have dogged you from your past and learned more positive ways of coping with them, you are free to be or do whatever you want. If you have done all the STEP UP actions throughout the book, I know that you are feeling a lot better about things than when you started. I'm praying that there was revelation in these pages for you and that you have managed to **Consider**, **Discover** and **Recover** from past issues that have been holding you back for years. I have shared bits of some of our girls' stories along the way. I would like to tell you where three of them are on their transformational journey right now. I've chosen these three because one moved her home to be near to Karis, another moved away completely, and the third chose to stay in the house with us. They are all living differently but are successful in their chosen areas.

One of our young ladies completed her time with us and didn't want to move back to her bungalow in the town where she came from as it was so far away. She felt she wanted to stay local because she had now made friends here. We managed to negotiate a housing association swap so that she could move into a little village just outside the town that Karis is based in.

She continued to run the Karis charity shop for a while after she left the house and helped out in Karis as a support worker. This helped her to consolidate her learning and made her emotionally stronger. When she decided what she would like to do in the future, she managed to get onto a three-year training course to be a paramedic. It took a while and there was a lot of competition, but she persevered. She has recently qualified and is now working locally with ambulances as a paramedic. Last year she trained for and ran the London Marathon, raising over £4,000 for Karis. While she occasionally has her struggles (who doesn't?) she is managing her life well and has a wide selection of good friends. She is involved with church and runs with her running club. She is still connected with Karis and continues to help, doing the banking and working with the girls on crafts sometimes. She is a great encouragement to the girls who see her and hear her story. It shows them what you can do if you keep making the right choices.

Another of our girls left Karis and moved to begin her training to work with children. It had been her heart's desire to do this for some time, but prior to her time at Karis she was too anxious to consider such a big step. The recruitment process for working with small children is rigorous, as you can imagine, but she was accepted for a place and is still in training there. She has stayed in contact with us and is doing well. She and her boyfriend are hoping to marry soon. Her most powerful way of dealing with her anxiety was the scripture she had written out because it really spoke to her. She still carries this around with her in case she needs it. In difficult moments she will get it out of her pocket and read it over to herself.

The final girl of these three finished the programme at Karis, but she decided not to move out as she no longer had a family home and didn't want to live by herself. She felt that Karis had become her home, and the other girls and staff her family, so she stayed with us. Once she finished the programme, she started her nursing training from Karis. Unfortunately, part way through she found it was becoming too much, so she took a break from the course. With a little more input from us over that time, she felt ready to pick up her training again the following year. Despite some quite traumatic family losses over the next two years she managed to finally complete her training. At the end of this she got a job in a unit specialising in neurological damage, similar to where her mother had been. She feels she can contribute to the families in this situation particularly well and wanted to do that because her own experiences during her mother's illness were negative. She still lives at Karis and helps to support the other girls.

It is encouraging to see how far these three have come. The other girls are doing well and are much further forward than when they started with us. It's not a quick process, though; we need to remember how long people sometimes live with damaged lives before they seek help.

Let's look at your life right now. How has your transformational healing journey gone? Well, I hope and pray. One of the reasons I suggest keeping a journal is so that you can go back over it at this stage and see your growth. Looking back to the beginning gives you a baseline so that you can measure how much you have achieved since you started this book. The girls often say that they read their old journal entries with surprise when they see how far they have come. I'm sure that will be the same for you.

The important thing to remember is that you are never doing this journey alone; God is always walking beside you. He prepared a plan for you before you were born, so you can be anything you set your heart on. It's likely He placed the desire in your heart in the first place – I know now that He did in mine. It is unlikely that my dream for Karis House would have worked if I had tried to do it using my own strength, but because it was His desire for me, somehow it works. I love that. He can make your dreams work, too. Dream big!

Summary

We have journeyed a long way together, and if you have done all the STEP UP actions in the book you will have come far. Learning to process things from your past is difficult but a necessary part of your healing journey. You may still have to go back to past chapters from time to time to pick out something that will help if an issue pops up unexpectedly. Don't be surprised or disappointed by that – we are all growing all the time. Just because you've done the hard work this time doesn't mean you'll never slip up again. Whatever happens next, though, you'll be better equipped to deal with it in the future because you will already have the tools. Don't crawl like a caterpillar when God has set you free to fly like a butterfly.

> 'I press on toward the goal to win the prize for which God has called me heavenward in Christ Jesus.'
> — Philippians 3:14

STEP UP actions

Spend time with God

Now is a good moment to spend some time with God. To do this, find a quiet space with no distractions and ask Him to bring to mind what He wants you to consider.

Think about what you've just read

Look at what we have covered throughout this journey and anything you may still need to work through to help in you in your recovery.

Explore the relevance to you

Write down anything that you have achieved during this journey, especially anything that was particularly important to you.

Pray about it

Let's pray to God to thank Him for being with you during this journey. Ask Him to be with you as you walk out transformed and ready to dream big. You can use the prayer below to get started or pray in your usual way to God, whichever feels most comfortable to you.

Father God, I thank You for travelling with me on my healing journey. Thank you for helping me to transform my life in such a mighty way. I pray that You would always be with me and that You would strengthen me as I move forward into everything else You have for me. Lord, help me to see clearly the purposes You have set before me for my future life. Thank you. Amen.

Uncover scriptures that speak to you

Write scriptures on Post-it notes or coloured card and put them all around the house or in your pocket to support your journey.

Personal journal

Write about the outcomes in your personal journal to remind you just how far you've come on the days when you need encouragement.

Conclusion

Well done. You have done some amazing work to get to the end of this book. At the beginning we were looking at who you were, and you had to consider all the things that could have formed you – who you were at that time. From there you had to consider how that had impacted how you felt about things. We then went on to consider what others see when they look at you. At the end of each chapter you did the STEP UP actions, which began your healing journey.

From there you had an opportunity to discover the coping strategies you have been using to manage day-to-day life. You were able to discover which of these could become more harmful than the things you were trying to escape from. Following that, there a chance to discover what else might have impacted you and how you could use safer options to keep yourself out of harm's way. There was an ongoing opportunity to learn more about yourself as the STEP UP actions came at the end of every chapter.

In the final section of the book, you worked on how to recover from the things you had discovered. You came to an understanding of how these had held you back from your dreams and were able to forgive people from your past who had caused you harm. You came to an acceptance of the things you cannot change and began to look forward to who you could now become. You recognised that, as a child of the living God, you are no longer alone and your deep desire to belong is met within the family of God. With a growing knowledge of who you are in Christ, you achieved real growth. Still keeping up the STEP UP actions, you finally came to the end of this healing journey.

My prayer for you is that you don't stop there. Keep walking with God, hear what He is telling you and continue to grow in your faith. Dream big, my friend, free now from all that held you back. You are no longer letting your past dictate your future but are transformed to live out God's purpose for your life. Go for it, secure in the knowledge that He is and always will be walking right beside you.

It would be fitting to end with the scripture we started with.

'Do not conform to the pattern of this world but be transformed by the renewing of your mind.'
— Romans 12:2

Congratulations! You have been transformed by the renewing of your mind. May God richly bless you as you continue your journey.

When you make the rest of your dreams a reality, please let me know about it, either on the Karis website (www.karishouse.com) or by emailing the address found at the back of the book. I would love to know how you are continuing to move forward.

Here are some words from one of the girls whose stories I tell that were written for this book:

'I never truly understood the impact my past life events had on me and how they impacted my current day thoughts and behaviours and how these had such an effect on my day-to-day living. I felt like I was in a hopeless situation unable to live a life worth living. It wasn't until I arrived at Karis, I started to see there was hope that I could recover and have a meaningful life. The journey was never easy or straightforward, but I wouldn't change it for the world. Through this journey I began to discover who I was in Christ and how my thoughts and behaviours had an impact not only on myself but those around me. Karis was my safe place to explore the reasons I had got to where I was and to practise my skills to change my thought processes and behaviours for the better. I now live my life fully for God and He has done more than I could ever have imagined.

If I could give advice to anyone who is in a similar place to where I was, it would be to dig into God, allow Him to direct your path and never put limits on what God can do for you. He is a healer, but you have to allow Him to work through you and those close to you for the incredible future He has planned for you to be revealed. Don't be scared to work through those things that scare you the most because behind them are where the biggest steps to your healing lie.'
— Former student at Karis House

Who Am I In Christ?

'Therefore, if anyone is in Christ, the new creation has come: The old has gone, the new is here!'
— 2 Corinthians 5:17

'God made Him who had no sin to be sin for us, so that in Him we might become the righteousness of God.'
— 2 Corinthians 5:21

'And God raised us up with Christ and seated us with Him in the heavenly realms in Christ Jesus.'
— Ephesians 2:6

'I no longer call you servants, because a
servant does not know his master's business.
Instead, I have called you friends, for everything that I learned from my Father I have
made known to you.'
— John 15:15

'For the Spirit God gave us does not make
us timid, but gives us power, love and self-
discipline.'
— 2 Timothy 1:7

'Therefore, since we have been justified
through faith, we have peace with God
through our Lord Jesus Christ.'
— Romans 5:1

'No, in all these things we are more than
conquerors through Him who loved us.'
— Romans 8:37

'In Him and through faith in Him we may
approach God with freedom and confidence.'
— Ephesians 3:12

'I praise you because I am fearfully and
wonderfully made; your works are wonderful,
I know that full well.'
— Psalm 139:14

'Yet to all who did receive Him to those who believed in his name, He gave the right to become children of God.'
— John 1:12

Just A Thought...

At this point we must consider that you may have uncovered some things that you think you need professional help with. If you are afraid to do that yourself, talk to a trusted friend. Please don't just try to cope with it alone. If there is no one you feel comfortable with, see if you feel able to talk to one of your leaders at church. If you're not sure which one, talk to the pastor, priest or vicar who will either help you or point you in the direction of the right leader for you. Another way to access help is to go and see your GP. They can refer you to someone appropriate, unless you can afford or would prefer a private or Christian counsellor. These can be found online, but check their credentials with the British Association for Counselling and Psychotherapy (BACP). Your GP can also refer you to the community mental health team in your area if that is more appropriate for you.

If you are a young woman between the ages of around eighteen and thirty-five you can check out the Karis House website (www.karishouse.com) to see if Karis might be appropriate for you. We have a referral process that starts with an email to us. You can self-refer or someone else can make the initial contact for you if you are too fearful at this stage. Again, don't just try to manage alone – help is out there.

There is an NHS webpage that gives a list of places to contact. You can find it at: www.nhs.uk/conditions/stress-anxiety-depression/mental-health-helplines

There are also some details below for organisations that can provide support.

Anxiety UK

Charity providing support if you have been diagnosed with an anxiety condition.

Phone: 03444 775 774 (Monday to Friday, 9.30am to 10pm; Saturday to Sunday, 10am to 8pm).

www.anxietyuk.org.uk

www.thecalmzone.net

Mind

Promotes the views and needs of people with mental health problems.

Phone: 0300 123 3393 (Monday to Friday, 9am to 6pm).

www.mind.org.uk

No Panic

Charity offering support for sufferers of panic attacks and obsessive-compulsive disorder (OCD). Offers a course to help overcome your phobia or OCD.

Phone: 0844 967 4848 (daily, 10am to 10pm). Calls cost 5p per minute plus your phone provider's access charge.

www.nopanic.org.uk

OCD UK

A charity run by and for people with OCD. Includes facts, news and treatments.

Phone: 0333 212 7890 (Monday to Friday, 9am to 5pm).

www.ocduk.org

PAPYRUS

Young suicide prevention society.

Phone: 0800 068 4141 (Monday to Friday, 10am to 10pm, and 2pm to 10pm on weekends and bank holidays).

www.papyrus-uk.org

Samaritans

Confidential support for people experiencing feelings of distress or despair.

Phone: 116 123 (free twenty-four-hour helpline).

www.samaritans.org

Refuge

Advice on dealing with domestic violence.

Phone: 0808 2000 247 (twenty-four-hour helpline).

www.refuge.org.uk

Alcoholics Anonymous

Phone: 0800 917 7650 (twenty-four-hour helpline).

www.alcoholics-anonymous.org.uk

Cruse Bereavement Care

Phone: 0808 808 1677 (Monday to Friday, 9am to 5pm).

www.cruse.org.uk

Rape Crisis

To find your local services, phone: 0808 802 9999 (daily, 12pm to 2.30pm and 7pm to 9.30pm).

www.rapecrisis.org.uk

Victim Support

Phone: 0808 168 9111 (twenty-four-hour helpline).

www.victimsupport.org

Beat

Charity formed to help those with eating disorders.

Phone: 0808 801 0677 (adults) or 0808 801 0711 (for under eighteens).

www.beateatingdisorders.org.uk

Acknowledgements

Firstly, it's only fitting that I honour all the beautiful, hurting girls that are brave enough to come to Karis House. Each of you had to come to the end of yourselves and ask for help, never an easy thing to do and yet you did it. You gave up everything you knew and moved to Lincolnshire to find your freedom. That is amazing, and as I see you all on arrival, anxious and fearful, I watch with wonder as God slowly opens your eyes and hearts to all He has for you. In return you blossom and grow, slowly understanding how your past is affecting you now and learning how to deal with it. Finally, you finish the programme and you leave us changed beyond all your expectations, confident and ready to take on the world. I love you all and thank God for the privilege He has given me in allowing me to be a small part of your journey.

I hope, dear reader, you will indulge me for a moment as I say a special thank you to one of our girls, Emily, who having fought so hard and overcome her emotional frailty, sadly finally succumbed to her precarious physical health. Even from your hospital bed you talked about Jesus, Em. You were a joy to have around – always a little ray of sunshine, looking out for others and making us laugh in the strangest moments. I still miss you, but at least you managed to achieve your beautiful wedding to your dream man. Rest in peace, sweetheart.

To you girls who allowed me to use parts of your stories as illustrations in this book, thank you. I believe your stories will have made things more accessible to those reading as hearing about how other people have been affected makes it more understandable. You know who you are even if no one else will. You have been doubly courageous sharing your stories firstly with us and then to help others. Well done and thank you.

Karis would not run but for the caring dedicated staff that work there. I could never do this alone; the work is emotionally demanding on every level and depends on each of us doing our part. You are brilliant, every one of you, bringing your own unique but Godly perspective. I thank you from the bottom of my heart for sharing in my dreams for the girls who come to us so broken and for seeing your role as a vocation, not a job, because that is what it is for certain.

Huge thanks go to my test readers who were kind enough to read my scrawly manuscript and with brilliant feedback help me to make this book what it is today. Writing the book was easy compared with having to actually allow someone else to read it, but you were very gentle with me and your suggestions were fabulous and added value. Thank you to Carly Wilkinson, Zoe Coleman, Charlotte Lovett, Charlotte Osborn, Susie Ramroop and last, but not least, my dear friend Marion Sandhu, who sort of started it all, in a way. One working lunch she decided I needed Jesus in my life and set about making sure that happened. The rest, as they say, is history. You have been my closest friend for more than twenty years now and I can't imagine my life without you. Your Godly support and encouragement on this book and working alongside me in the charity are invaluable, thank you.

Elisabeth, being your Mum has given me the greatest pleasure. My life changed for the better the moment you were born. I am proud beyond measure of the incredible things you have achieved already and am in awe of what you are capable of, I know you will do even greater things yet. Thank you for your ongoing encouragement throughout this process and all the marketing and fundraising you do in support of the charity. I don't know how you find the time while running your own business, it's amazing.

Without a doubt my husband, Mike, is a superstar. He has tolerated the constant chatter about 'my book' which to be honest neither of us were sure would actually happen. He never complained about my endless hours at the computer appearing only for meals, which he of course cooked fantastically, having grown many of the vegetables and fruit contained therein himself. I would possibly have written my book without him, but I would have definitely snacked on junk food rather than cooking, leaving me pretty unhealthy by now. Thank you for attending to absolutely everything in such a loving and thoughtful way and being so incredibly supportive, not just of the book but in every area of my life.

Lucy McCarraher, Joe Gregory and the brilliant team at Rethink Press. You have been amazing, it's so fantastic to work with such a professional team. You have shown a genuine interest in getting my book right for *me* from the very start. Lucy is so unassuming, yet she is packed to the brim with knowledge about writing and has incredible communication abilities that skilfully steer you through the whole process. All your fears and anxieties she addresses almost before you recognise they're there, holding you accountable in a gentle but firm way that is hard to argue with. She has certainly been one of the key reasons that this book is out there now, thank you so much, Lucy.

Finally, I want to thank you for reading my book. I hope that you have enjoyed it and you have grown through it. My hope is that with fresh understanding you are now free from all that held you back and you are no longer letting your past dictate your future, transformed to live out God's purpose for your life. I would really love to hear all about your progress, why not drop me an email to let me know how you're doing?

Only fitting, however, that the very last word belongs to God.

Thank you Lord that you ordained my purpose before I was born and that you trust me with this amazing calling. I feel so privileged every day to serve such a gracious and loving God in this way. Thank you, Lord. Amen.

The Author

Jenny has a wide-ranging background in the NHS including district nursing, management in nursing, clinical risk, and speech and language therapy, finally ending her time in the NHS as Assistant Director of Public Health in Lincolnshire. During this period she worked with and learned a lot about people from all areas, both colleagues and patients. In 2009 she left the NHS to set up a charity to offer supported living accommodation to young people with problems, who seemed to be falling between the gaps of what little help was available.

Throughout her time in health, and subsequently her charity, Jenny has also been a Leader in the church. She started her leadership roles with the Youth Group but is now involved in many areas including events, worship band and pastoral care, and she enjoys preaching whenever possible. As a Trustee of the church, she is also on the Senior Leadership Team.

All these experiences combine to give her a rich understanding of people and a passion for the gospel which she believes can change lives, resulting in the birth of Karis House. This book is to help expand this vision so that more lives will be transformed by the love of God.

If you or someone you know may benefit from Karis House, contact Karis House:

✉ info@karishouse.com

🌐 www.karishouse.com

📘 The Lighthouse Project, Spalding

If you would like someone to come and speak to a group, contact the author:

✉ jenny@jennytedbury.com

🌐 www.jennytedbury.com

🌐 www.allalittlebitbroken.com